ISBN: 978129011408

Published by:
HardPress Publishing
8345 NW 66TH ST #2561
MIAMI FL 33166-2626

Email: info@hardpress.net
Web: http://www.hardpress.net

CATALOGUES
FREE

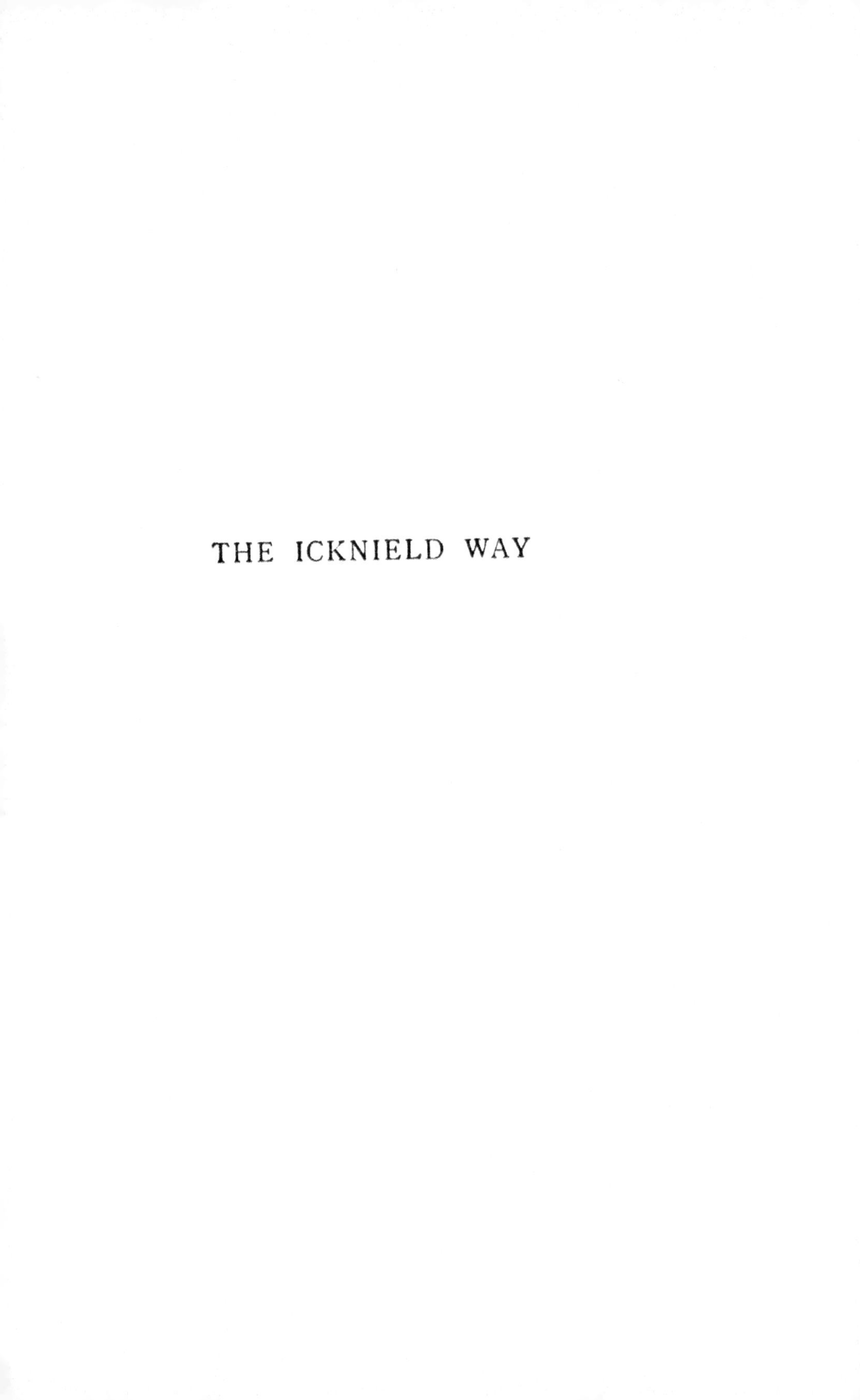

THE ICKNIELD WAY

UNIFORM WITH THIS VOLUME

THE OLD ROAD

By HILAIRE BELLOC

Illustrated by WILLIAM HYDE

THE STANE STREET

By HILAIRE BELLOC

Illustrated by WILLIAM HYDE

THE FOREST OF DEAN

By ARTHUR O. COOKE

Illustrated by J. W. KING

Streatley Mill and Church

THE ICKNIELD WAY

BY
EDWARD THOMAS

WITH ILLUSTRATIONS BY
A. L. COLLINS

LONDON
CONSTABLE & COMPANY LTD.
1916

DEDICATION

TO HARRY HOOTON

When I sat down at the "Dolau Cothi Arms" this evening I remembered my dedication to you. You said I could dedicate this book to you if I would make a real dedication, not one of my shadowy salutes befitting shadows rather than men and women. It seems odd you should ask thus for a sovereign's worth of—shall I say?—English prose from a writer by trade. But though I turn out a large, if insufficient, number of sovereigns' worths, and am become a writing animal, and could write something or other about a broomstick, I do not write with ease: so let that difficulty give the dedication its value.

It is right that I should remember you upon a walk, for I have walked more miles with you than with anyone else except myself. While I walked you very often danced, on the roads of Kent, Sussex, Surrey, and Hampshire. This evening when I went out on the Sarn Helen everybody was in chapel, I think, unless it was the Lord, for he also seemed to me to be walking in the cool. I was very much alone, and glad to be. You were a ghost, and not a man of fourteen stone, and I thought that perhaps after all that shadowy salute would be fittest. But I have put my pen to paper: I have set out and I will come to an end; for, as I said, I am a writing animal. In the days of those old walks I could have written a dedication in Norfolk-jacket style, all about "the open road," and the search for something "over the hills and far away": I should have reminded you at some length how Borrow stayed at this inn, and that Dolau Cothi is the house where he could have lived with satisfaction "if backed by a couple of thousands a year." To-day I know there is nothing beyond the farthest of far ridges except a signpost to unknown places. The end is in the means—in the sight of that beautiful long straight line of the Downs in which a curve is latent—in the houses we shall never enter, with their dark secret windows and quiet hearth smoke, or their ruins friendly only to elders and nettles—in the people passing whom we shall never know though we may love them. To-day I know that I walk because it is necessary to do so in order both to live and to make a living. Once those walks might have made a book; now they make a smile or a sigh, and I am glad they are in ghostland and not fettered in useless print. This book for you was to have been a country book, but I see that it has turned out to be another of those books made out of books founded on other books. Being but half mine it can only be half yours, and I owe you an apology as well as a dedication. It is, however, in some ways a fitting book for me to write. For it is about a road which begins many miles before I could come on its traces and ends miles beyond where I had to stop. I could find no excuse for supposing it to go to Wales and following it there into the Ceidrych Valley, along the Towy to Caermarthen, and so to St. David's which is now as holy as Rome, though once only a third as holy. Apparently no special mediæval use revived it throughout its course, or gave it a new entity like that of the Pilgrims' Way from Winchester to Canterbury that you and I walked on many a time—by the "Cock" at Detling, the "Black Horse" at Thurnham, the "King's Head" (once, I believe, the "Pilgrims' Rest") at Hollingbourne, above Harrietsham, past Deodara Villas, above Lenham and Robert Philpot's "Woodman's Arms," and so on to Eastwell; always among beech and yew and Canterbury bells, and always over the silver of whitebeam leaves. I could not find a beginning or an end of the Icknield Way. It is thus a symbol of mortal things with their beginnings and ends always in immortal darkness. I wish the book had a little more of the mystery of the road about it. You at least will make allowances—and additions; and God send me many other readers like you. And as this is the bottom of the sheet, and ale is better than ink, though it is no substitute, I label this "Dedication," and wish you with me inside the "Dolau Cothi Arms" at Pumpsaint, in Caermarthenshire.

EDWARD THOMAS.

NOTE

I HAVE to acknowledge the very great kindness of Mr. Hilaire Belloc, Mr. Harold T. E. Peake, and Mr. R. Hippisley Cox while I was writing this book, though I do so with some hesitation, because I may seem to make them responsible for some of my possible mistakes and certain shortcomings. A man could hardly have three better guides than Mr. Belloc for his grasp and sympathy with roads, Mr. Peake for his caution and curiosity, and "documents, documents!" and Mr. Cox for his ardour and familiarity with trodden turf; and I must add my testimony to that of my betters to the merits of Mr. Belloc's *Old Road*, Mr. Peake's chapter on prehistoric roads in *Memorials of Old Leicestershire*, and Mr. Cox's *Avebury*. To Mr. Peake I am indebted not only for suggestions that were invaluable to me, notably in the matter of the Ridgeway and the Bishop of Cloyne's pernicious theory, but for the use of his copies of the greater part of the materials of my second chapter. I have also had great kindness from the Rev. E. H. Goddard and Mr. W. Gough.

EDWARD THOMAS.

LLAUGHARNE,
CAERMARTHENSHIRE.

CONTENTS

CONTENTS

LIST OF ILLUSTRATIONS

THE ICKNIELD WAY

THE ICKNIELD WAY

CHAPTER I

ON ROADS AND FOOTPATHS

MUCH has been written of travel, far less of the road. Writers have treated the road as a passive means to an end, and honoured it most when it has been an obstacle; they leave the impression that a road is a connection between two points which only exists when the traveller is upon it. Though there is much travel in the Old Testament, "the way" is used chiefly as a metaphor. "Abram journeyed, going on still toward the south," says the historian, who would have used the same words had the patriarch employed wings. Yet to a nomadic people the road was as important as anything upon it. The earliest roads wandered like rivers through the land, having, like rivers, one necessity, to keep in motion. We still say that a road "goes" to London, as we "go" ourselves. We point out a white snake on a green hill-side, and tell a man: "That is going to Chichester." At our inn we think when recollecting the day: "That road must have

B

gone to Strata Florida." We could not attribute more life to them if we had moving roads with platforms on the sidewalks. We may go or stay, but the road will go up over the mountains to Llandovery, and then up again over to Tregaron. It is a silent companion always ready for us, whether it is night or day, wet or fine, whether we are calm or desperate, well or sick. It is always going: it has never gone right away, and no man is too late. Only a humorist could doubt this, like the boy in a lane who was asked: "Where does this lane go to, boy?" and answered: "I have been living here these sixteen years and it has never moved to my knowledge." Some roads creep, some continue merely; some advance with majesty, some mount a hill in curves like a soaring sea-gull.

Even as towns are built by rivers, instead of rivers being conducted past towns, so the first settlements grew up alongside roads which had formerly existed simply as the natural lines of travel for a travelling race. The oldest roads often touch the fewest of our modern towns, villages, and isolated houses. It has been conjectured that the first roads were originally the tracks of animals. The elephant's path or tunnel through the jungle is used as a road in India to-day, and in early days the wild herds must have been invaluable for making a way through forest, for showing the firmest portions of bogs and lowland marshes, and for suggesting fords. The herd would wind according to the conditions of the land and to inclinations of many inexplicable kinds, but the winding of the road would be no disadvantage to men who found their living by the wayside, men to whom time was not money. Roads which grew thus by nature and by necessity appear to be almost as lasting as rivers. They are found fit for the uses of countless different generations of men outside cities, because, apart from cities and their needs, life changes little. If they go out of use in a new or a changed civilization, they may still be frequented by men of the most primitive habit. All over England may be found old roads, called Gypsy Lane, Tinker's Lane, or Smuggler's Lane; east of Calne, in Wiltshire, is a Juggler's Lane; and as if the ugliness of the "uggle" sound pleased the good virtuous country folk, they have got a Huggler's Hole a little west of Semley and south of Sedgehill in the same county: there are also Beggar's Lanes and roads leading past places called Mock Beggar, which is said to mean Much Beggar. These little-used roads are known to lovers, thieves, smugglers, and ghosts. Even if long neglected they are not easily obliterated. On the fairly even and dry ground of the high ridges where men and cattle could spread out wide as they journeyed, the earth itself is unchanged by centuries of traffic, save that the grass is made finer, shorter, paler, and more numerously starred with daisies. But on the slopes down to a plain or ford the road takes its immortality by violence, for it is divided into two or three or a score of narrow courses, trenched so deeply that they might often seem to be the work rather of some fierce natural force than of slow - travelling men, cattle, and pack-horses. The name Holloway, or Holway, is therefore a likely sign of an old road. So is Sandy Lane, a name in which lurks the half-fond contempt of country people for the road which a good "hard road" has superseded, and now little used save in bird's-nesting or courting days. These old roads will endure as long as the Roman streets, though great is the difference between the unraised trackway, as dim as a wind-path on the sea, and the straight embanked Roman highway which made the proverb "Plain as Dunstable Road," or "Good plain Dunstable"—for Watling Street goes broad and straight through that town. Scott has one of these ghostly old roads in *Guy Mannering*. It was over a heath that had Skiddaw and Saddleback for background, and he calls it a *blind road*—"the track so slightly marked by the passengers' footsteps that it can but be traced by a slight shade of verdure from the darker heath around it, and, being only visible to the eye when at some distance, ceases to be distinguished while the foot is actually treading it."

The making of such roads seems one of the most natural operations of man, one in which he least conflicts with nature and the animals. If he makes roads outright and rapidly, for a definite purpose, they may perish as rapidly, like the new roads of modern Japanese enterprise, and their ancient predecessors live on to smile at their ambition. These are the winding ways preferred by your connoisseur to-day. "Give me," says Hazlitt, "the clear blue sky over my head and the green turf beneath my feet, a winding road before me, and a three-hours' march to dinner—and then to thinking!" These windings are created by the undulating of the land, and by obstacles like those of a river—curves such as those in the High Street of Oxford, which Wordsworth called "the stream-like windings of that glorious street." The least obstacle might bring about a loop, if nothing more, and as even a Roman road curled round Silbury Hill, so the path of the Australian savage is to be seen twisting round bush after bush as if it enjoyed the interruption, though it cannot purl like the river at a bend. Probably these twists, besides being unconsciously adapted to the lie of the land, were, as they are still, easeful and pleasant to the rover who had some natural love of journeying. Why go straight? There is nothing at the end of any road better than may be found beside it, though there would be no travel did men believe it. The straight road, except over level and open country, can only be made by those in whom extreme haste and forethought have destroyed the power of joy, either at the end or at any part of its course. Why, then, go straight? The connoisseur had something of the savage in him when he demanded a winding road.

It is not, however, to a man walking for pleasure that we shall go for a sense of roads, but to one like Bunyan. *Pilgrim's Progress* is full of the sense of roads. See Christian going to Mr. Legality's house. It is a mountain road, and the hill overhangs it so much that he is afraid to venture further "lest the hill should fall on his head." When Goodwill points out the narrow way, he says it was "cast up by the patriarchs, prophets, Christ, and his Apostles," i.e. made into a raised track bounded by ditches from which the earth was cast up to form the embankment. When Christian comes to the Hill Difficulty you see the primitive man deciding to go straight uphill, turning not to the left by the way called Danger into a great wood, nor to the right to Destruction and the "wide field full of dark mountains." How full of plain English country wayfaring is the passage where Hopeful and Christian take a road by a river-side, and then when it turns away from the water they see a stile leading into a path which keeps on, as a path would do, along the bank through By-path Meadow: only, as it happens, the river is in flood and they must turn back again towards the stile. This man knew roads, and one of his temptations after conversion was to try his faith by bidding the puddles on the road between his own village and Bedford to be dry. Cervantes had the sense of roads. He begins, indeed, by making Don Quixote sally forth "upon the plain" like any knight of chivalry "pricking o'er the plain" and taking the way chosen by his horse because thus would adventures best be compassed; but it is upon a road that he and most of his knights, ladies, and enchanters travel. Malory's book would have less vitality in its marvel if it were not for the roads: the three highways, for example, where Sir Marhaus and Sir

Gawaine and Sir Uwaine were to separate for their adventures each with his damosel ; and the wild ways of Sir Launcelot when he "rode many wild ways, throughout marches and many wild ways," until he came to a valley and a knight therein with a naked sword chasing a lady. *Cymbeline* again, and some of the historical plays of Shakespeare, give a grand impression of wide tracts of country traversed by roads of great purpose and destiny.

More often in books we move, as I have said, from place to place as in a dream. But it is a dream in the *Mabinogion* which gives one of the most majestic scenes of travel. I mean the dream of the Emperor Maxen. He dreamed that he was journeying along a river valley towards its source, and up over the highest mountain in the world until he saw mighty rivers descending to the sea, and one of them he followed to a great city at its mouth and a vast castle in the city. At the end of his journey the dreaming Emperor found a girl so beautiful that when he awoke he could think of naught else, while years went by, except her beauty. He sent out pioneers to discover the road of his dream, and at last they brought him to the castle and the same girl Helen sitting in the hall of it. She became his bride, and he gave her three castles—one at Arvon in North Wales, one at Caerleon, and one at Caermarthen in the South. Then, says the tale, "Helen bethought her to make high-roads from one castle to another throughout the Island of Britain. And the roads were made. And for this cause are they called the roads of Helen Luyddawc, that she was sprung from a native of this island, and the men of the Island of Britain would not have made these great roads for any save her." It is natural to connect with this Helen the great ancient roads leading north and south across Wales known as Sarn Helen or Elen. Nothing could be more noble as the name of a mountain road than Sarn Helen or Helen's Causeway. It suggests to the ordinary fanciful and unhistoric mind the British Helena, mother of the Emperor Constantine, and that it suggested this long ago is clear from the old identification of Helen Luyddawc with the only child of King Cole of Colchester. The name has more recently been explained as Sarn y Lleng, the Road of the Legions. Sir John Rhys[1] insists upon Elen instead of Helen, and believes her to be one of the pagan goddesses of the dusk. "There is," he says, "a certain poetic propriety in associating the primitive paths and roads of the country with this vagrant goddess of dawn and dusk." These wandering paths are to the hard white highways what dusk is to the full blaze of day. First perhaps trodden by the wild herd and still without terrors for it, they might well be protected by a sort of Artemis, goddess of wildernesses and of forked ways, kind both to human hunters and the wild quarry. They belong to the twilight of the world. No doubt the sun shines no brighter at noon than it did then on a perfectly wild earth, on flowers that were never gathered, on bright plumage that no man had coveted. But all the forest and marsh of primeval earth form in the

[1] Hibbert Lectures, 1889, p. 16.

imagination mists to which the lack of history adds yet another veil. These mists lie over the world, to my mind, exactly as the white mist of summer lies, turning into a sea most of what once was land and making islands of the woods on the steep, uncultivated tracts. The islands rising out of the mists of time are the hills and mountains, and along their ridges ran the first roads, and by them are the squares and circles of the first habitations and the mounds of the first solemnized graves, used sometimes, it is thought, as guides for travellers.

It is particularly easy to think of Southern England as several chains of islands, representing the Downs, the Chilterns and Gog Magogs, the Mendips, Cotswolds and Quantocks. I have more than once caught myself thinking of the broad elephantine back of Butser Hill heaving up, spotted with gorse but treeless, between Petersfield and Portsmouth, as Ararat, though my unfaithful eyes fail to imagine the ark. There are days now when the clear suddenly swelling hills like Tarberry or Barrow Hill in Hampshire, or Cley Hill or the Knolls of Maiden Bradley in Wiltshire, or the abrupt promontories like Chanctonbury or Noar Hill near Selborne, or the long trooping ranges, seem to be islands or atolls looming dimly through the snowy still mists of morning or the clouds of rainstorm. Even without mist some of the isolated green hills rise out of the pale levels of cornland as out of sea ; and I have seen, from near Bruton, the far-distant mass of Cadbury, the hill some call Camelot in Somerset, look like a dark precipitous isle. When the early roads along the ridges were made, the hills still more closely resembled islands emerging out of the forest and out of the marsh. The watersheds created the roads, as they still do over hundreds of miles in Africa. The roads keep to the highland, and if this highland were to form a circle they would follow it; and hunters say, as Mr. H. W. Nevinson tells us in *A Modern Slavery*, that the elephants do "move in a kind of rough zone or circle—from the Upper Zambesi across the Cuando into Angola and the district where they passed me, and so across the Cuanza northward and eastward into the Congo, and round towards Katanga and the sources of the Zambesi again." Somewhere too I have met the tradition, probably a Welsh one, that this island of Britain was girdled by a road above its shores. The early nomads would descend from the ridges only with reluctance, for fear of the marsh and the dim forest. Doubtless their travelling oxen, especially if burdened, had the same horror of mud—when they are not free to wallow in it—as they have to-day. In a very early age it is likely that men would go down to the rivers only to water their cattle, and then return to the heights. There would be several drinking-places, and at one of them they would discover a ford, unless the animals had already marked one, and then if the river had not become a boundary they might cross and continue their wanderings along a road upon the next island of hills. Thus island would be joined to island. The paths ran along the back of each one and branched over the spurs, and the linking up of these would tend to form highways of great length, like that trodden by Launcelot, "far o'er the long backs of the bushless downs" to Camelot. It were easy to take such a route to-day from anywhere in Berkshire or Hampshire, travelling high and away from

The Ridgeway, near Blowingstone Hill, Berkshire.

cities, except cities of the dead like Avebury, far from towns and villages, through Wiltshire into Somerset or Dorset, on roads which are altogether turf or have so goodly a border of grass and blossom that the wayfarer need never touch the hard white grit which is the same on a metalled road whether in London or in wild country.

Down from the realm-long bridge of islands above

the world the traveller descended to cities of men. Thus Sir Launcelot after long riding in a great forest came into a low country of fair rivers and meadows and saw before him the long bridge and the three pavilions on it, " of silk and sendal of divers hue." Thus Sir Bevis of Hampton, cheated of his patrimony by a cruel mother and keeping sheep on the Downs, looked and saw below him the town and the tower that should have been his. Thus Cobbett, looking from Portsdown Hill above Portsmouth, saw the sea for the first time and the English fleet riding at anchor at Spithead and his heart " was inflated with national pride," and though he had walked thirty miles that day he slept not a moment, but rose at daylight and offered himself for the sea on board the *Pegasus*. Thus we descend on Winchester or Salisbury out of the hills, glad to get there what we want as we have for many days gladly wanted what we could get. It has been, let us say, a day that should be spring, and in the dark, wet copses there were thousands of primroses. All day the wind, and often rain and wind together, roared in the trees. The pale flowers were soaked and frayed and speckled with dust from the trees, and they hung down or were broken from their soft stalks. But the high land and the neighbouring sky exalt us. Even the sight of these tender-blubbering petals ruined in the drenched grass was pleasant. We should have liked better to see them unspoiled and wide in the sun ; but we did not wish them to be so, and their distress did but add to the glory of the storm and to our defiance, just as did the cowering of birds, of bowed trees, of whole woods, under the wild, shadowy swoop of the mist and rain, and the valleys below us humbled, their broad fields, their upthrust churches and clustered villages overwhelmed and blotted out, and everything annihilated save the wind, the rain, the streaming road, and the vigorous limbs and glowing brain and what they created. Not that we did not welcome freely the minutes of dimly shining stillness that were as a secluded garden in a city, when the storm paused; for then we drank in the blue sky and the dark revealed tracts of plain and hill that lay stunned and astonished like a dreamer opening his eyelids after tumultuous dreams; we drank them with easy joy as of a man reading a great adventure when the heroes of it have long been dead, for we ourselves were so much above all that expanse which, powerless and quiet, might almost seem to belong to the past or to a tale. We and the storm were one and we were triumphant; and in mid triumph we came down to the lighted streets.

As the first roads were made by men following herds, either as hunters or as herdsmen, so ox and sheep have long helped to keep them up. The great road of pilgrimage from Damascus to Mecca is not a made road, but composed of the parallel strands of old hollow camel paths. These, says Mr. Charles M. Doughty in *Arabia Deserta*, "one of the ancient Arabian poets has compared to the bars of the rayed Arabic mantle." To our own day in England drovers took the cattle lazily along the old roads of the watersheds and ridges. "Ox Drove" is the name in several places of an old green road. Travellers in Wiltshire have noticed on the one-inch Ordnance Survey Map a "British Trackway" running W.S.W. out of the road from the Deverills to Maiden Bradley. A large tumulus stands in the first field, as if for a sign at the beginning of the track. Locally this is known as the "Ox Road," and is said to have been used by droves coming from Mid and East Somerset. It is a continuation of the hard road which it leaves at the tumulus, and following it and its continuations you may travel through Kilmington, and between the Jack's Castle tumulus and King Alfred's tower, down Kingsettle Hill, and on close to Cadbury Castle, to Ilchester, and, joining the Foss Way, reach Devon and Cornwall. Only one mile of its course is marked in Old English letters "British Trackway," and this is apparently not even a path, but a protracted unevenness of the ground, sometimes almost amounting to a ridge or terrace in the grass, for the most part following the hedges, and in one place entering a short, nettly lane. The road, in spite of its romantic Old English lettering, is at this point a very humble specimen of an ancient road and ox drove; for it goes through meadows which are low compared with the fine waves of Down—White Sheet Downs and the Maiden Bradley Hills—on either side of it. A far better one is the ox drove which this joins at Kilmington. It is said to have been used as a road from London to Exeter. Farmers will tell you that the Ox Drove "never touched water," which they will qualify by saying you could go from Monkton Deverill to Marlborough without touching water or crossing it, and if that also is impossible, at any rate they have the tradition of the road's character in their heads, seldom as they may use it. Along it, says Mr. J. U. Powell,[1] came " fat cattle from the Somerset pastures to London," and once he thinks it was a road leading to the lead of Somerset and tin of Cornwall.

It goes through the orchards of Somerset as a good hard road, but often deprived of its right green borders. When these have been lost they have not always disappeared, and its old breadth is shown probably by a long, narrow field lying first on one side and then, after a zigzag, on the other, as near the " Bull " to the east of Bruton. Sometimes with a green space beside the road, or a depression behind the hedge, or an aimless avenue of oak trees as at Redlynch, marking the old course, it is a narrow road going in a determined manner up and down, but with few deviations and having a purpose obviously unconnected with the few cottages on its edge. Here it is called the Hardway. The " hard road " is the countryman's admiring term for a made road; but it is suggested that the Hardway is the Har- or Harrow-Way, and is a continuation of a road running east and west through Hampshire and Wiltshire. It crosses the little shaded river Brue and ascends Kingsettle Hill between high banks of beech and oak and bluebell. It mounts, like a savage who does not mind

[1] *Wiltshire Archæological Magazine*, XXXIV.

being out of breath, straight up the steep wooded wall of the hill until at the top it is eight hundred and fifty feet high instead of four hundred, and takes you into Wiltshire. On the right is the huge square tower of brick erected by one of the Colt Hoare family in honour of King Alfred. The name Kingsettle Hill was thought by Colt Hoare to mark the pass of King Alfred when, with the chief men of Somerset, he issued from Athelney "after Eastertide," in 878, and marched to Egbert's stone in the east part of Selwood Forest. This "stone" or "cliff" has been supposed to be White Sheet Hill, a very conspicuous and noble place for the King to gather the people of Somerset, Wiltshire, and Hampshire before leading them to the victory of Edington. On the right and, like Alfred's Tower, at the brink of the hill is the big tumulus known as Jack's Castle; and from either you command Somersetshire nearly as far as the curvature of the earth allows. From the oaks and bluebells of the slopes beneath you stretches a low subdivided country of many oaks—and cuckoos calling from them—and the Hardway penetrating it from the south-west. Colt Hoare calls the tumulus "Selwood Barrow," a beacon above the great Forest of Selwood and possibly a direction post for travellers from the west to Old Sarum. In the north-west the land rises up to a ridge with a comb of beech trees, which is Creech Hill above Bruton, and at its feet the masses of Pink Wood and Norridge Wood. The Mendips are a dim cloud beyond it on the right, the Quantocks a dimmer cloud on the left; and in the low land between them is Athelney, and near it Glastonbury, standing above the full-grown Brue. Sometimes the wind-like sound of an invisible train ascends.

The road takes you through the remains of Selwood Forest. Now it has a fair green border, often of considerable breadth. That you are in Wiltshire there can be no doubt on emerging from the trees. For in front upon the left are those gentle monsters, the smooth Long and Little Knolls above Maiden Bradley, smooth, detached green dunes crested and fringed with beeches. Under this side of the Long Knoll is the tower of Kilmington Church among its trees. Lying across the road a few miles ahead are the bare White Sheet Downs, which are to be mounted, and farther to the right the wooded beacons above Fonthill Gifford and East Knoyle. The road makes for the scar of a high quarry on the nearest slope of White Sheet, a little to the left of a lesser isolated hill, a smooth, wooded knoll or islet. The road is gently and evenly rising, a hard, white road almost straight, between grassy borders with thorns and brambles under beeches that overhang from behind the hedge. They are good trees standing on a strip of turf furrowed as if it had once been the road or part of it; and some young ones have been lately planted, so that all is not yet over with English country, though landlords say so. The road crosses another to Kilmington and Yarnfield, and at once it is older-looking, hard, but winding slightly among bushy and lush steep banks. You see flowers and ash trees, and a linnet on the tip of one, but nothing distant save white clouds and the blue. Here it is called Long Lane, and among its herbage is an old London milestone. Long Lane is often the title of a lane coming from somewhere afar off: there is one south of Hermitage, giving its name to a village, in Berkshire, and one near Cucklington in Somerset, where there is a Tinker's Hill also. In another mile Long Lane crosses the Maiden Bradley road by a smithy and a "Red Lion"; its name becomes White Sheet Lane, and it goes straight in sight of the high white quarry and the deep tracks up to White Street Castle. Like Long Lane, it is a parish boundary. Both are without a house: the road has hardly passed a house since Redlynch, save at a crossing, and those living in the houses use the road only for a mile or so on the way to a village on either side. Slanting uphill under the quarry, with a parallel green way hollowed beside it, goes the road's bolder self. The hedges and banks are low, and the cornland or meadow is open round about. The lane turns to climb White Sheet Hill, and beeches and some whitebeam trees cool the beginning of the ascent; there are myriads of primroses in their season and chaffinches singing. You pass a thatched house and the lime-kiln of "Tom Gatehouse, Lime Burner," by the quarry, and another milestone showing twenty-three miles to Sarum and a date like 1757—when Blake was born. Looking back, the Knolls are on the right and Alfred's Tower on the left among the woods. There are tumuli on the right as the road comes clear out on to the hill-top and travels between the wired fences of the downland pasture. Here stand cows who do not often see a pencil sharpened. Pewits wheel over and before and behind ; all along the high course of the road the pewits cry and wheel. The road is at first rutted, but is soon a green smooth track on the highest land, skirting the upper ends of coombes dappled dusky gold by gorse, and commanding bare downland on the left and wooded hills on the right, and looking along a great bottom to the church tower of Mere, and Mere's beautiful "Long Hill," and the wide-arboured vale stretching away to the long ridge of Dorset. It is a high way and a proud way. After crossing an ancient ditch it is labelled "British Trackway," and ahead it is seen going between a wire fence and a dark line of tussocks. Then it is divided into three or four parallel terraces grooved by wheels, but with a lark's nest in the green rut. It crosses the Mere road as two hollow ways side by side, but in a little while is only a green track with single thorns on the left. Here is the twenty-first milestone from Sarum, the ninety-ninth from London, inscribed 1750, and it is called the London Drove Road ; it is still in sight of Alfred's Tower, now protruding above White Sheet ramparts. In one place it is so wide that the milestone stands out in the middle, like a traveller asleep or turned to stone among mole-heaps that have blotted the signs of other travellers. On the left, as far as the main Wincanton road, part of the track is embanked ; entering the hard motor road to Amesbury and London, the old way is outlined chiefly by the thorns of Old Willoughby Hedge on the left. The road going hedgeless across the downland is but the thin backbone of the old green way. For a time the line of thorns diverges, and then, soon after the crossing of the Warminster road, they come slanting from the right to meet the road and cross it just before another milestone. Hereby are three milestones on different roads, all close together, which has caused the easy winning of merry wagers to run past three milestones in three minutes. The drove crosses several roads going to Hindon, as a broad green track with or without a hedge, marked by its greater profusion of daisies and its paleness and lack of tussocks. Still there are pewits, and somewhere not far away a Pewit Castle. It is joined again by the main Amesbury road beyond Cold Berwick Hill, but presently deserted, the busier white way going boldly off over the ridge, and down to the Wylye River and up again on to Salisbury Plain by Yarnbury, and so past Stonehenge to Amesbury. The green road winds along the south slope of the ridge. Now two lines of thorns show the course far ahead, or the white weals of an ascent are seen; now gorse encroaches on it, and at a crossway corned-beef tins and grey embers mark an encampment of nomads. It passes thickets of thorn and wayfaring trees burying an old milestone to Sarum. Turf or corn lies on either hand or on both. It keeps along the edge of Groveley Woods and within sound of the nightingales until it bends down to Salisbury; once probably it or a higher parallel course went over a ford to Old Sarum, and evidently it is vastly older than the eighteenth-century milestones, perhaps old enough to have guided the Hampshire men and some of the Wiltshiremen to Alfred, a road such as Cobbett loved for the hammering of horses' hoofs on flints.

Another fine ox drove, and dignified by that name and by old lettering on the Ordnance Map, ran clear for a long stretch along the high land south of the Ebble River, from a point four miles south of Salisbury and westwards by Winkelbury to the south of Shaftesbury. It may some day be proved that one of the most famous of ancient roads, the Icknield Way itself, was an ox drove. There is said to be a charter mentioning the Icknield Way as "the way the cattle go"; and one writer has boldly derived the very name from the British Yken, or Ychen, meaning oxen. Every district in the chalk country has its tradition of an old road, now surviving in a footpath or in broken vertebræ of lane and footpath to provide walkers with endless theories. At Swindon, for example, it is said[1] that the Holy Well stood on a road coming from the east and going westward past Bradenstoke Abbey into Somerset, and on another used by pilgrims to the shrine of St. Anne's in the Wood, at Brislington in Somerset, which went by Elcombe, Hay Lane Bridge, Bushton, Clyffe, Calne, Studley, Chippenham, Pewsham Forest, Bradford, Keynsham Abbey, and Whitchurch, to Brislington, which is in the south-east of Bristol and has now a station called

[1] *Swindon Fifty Years Ago*, by William Morris.

St. Ann's Park. But this is not the place to give way to the fascination of a roll-call of country names.

Except that bridges superannuated fords, the conditions for the travelling of cattle cannot have changed much from Alfred's time until the day of railway trucks carrying thickets of moaning horns and square blocks of sheep. The turnpike system helped to preserve the old roads because drovers using them could avoid the tolls; their cattle could also feed by the wayside. Canon Jackson,[1] in 1862, said that the Ridgeway of Berkshire and Wiltshire was part of the road used for ages and to this day for driving cattle from Anglesey into Kent. Mr. Walter Money, in a note to Miss Gossett's *Shepherds of Britain*, said much the same thing. Unfortunately neither has told us anything of their route. I have no doubt they could have covered most of the distance on grass. I should like to have travelled with them. You will find "Welsh Ways" all over England. Walkers or Workaway Hill, where the Ridgeway descends southward from Wansdyke to the Pewsey Valley, is said to be a corruption of Weala-wege, and to have been called Walcway (or Welshway) by a shepherd not long ago. There is a "Welshway" in Northamptonshire making past Northampton for Wales by way of Banbury and the Cotswolds, and said to have been the route of Welsh drovers. There is a "Welsh Lane" in the Cotswolds turning out of the Gloucester road, three or four miles from Cirencester, and going up the

[1] *Wiltshire Archæological Magazine*, VII, 125.

Under Liddington Hill, Wiltshire.

hill by Four Mile Bottom towards Barnsley. I met an old man who remembered helping the Welsh drovers with their black cattle there sixty years ago. They were putting up near by for the night, and they liked the boy because his name was David. In the downland these roads would be practicable for the most part all the year round; but Defoe tells us that the clay roads of the Midlands used to be so bad that graziers sold their stock in September and October: they could then be taken to the neighbourhood of London and kept until midwinter to be sold at a high price. Cheshire men used to send their cheese to London either all the way by sea or overland to Burton, and so by the river to Hull and thence by sea. Gloucester men sent their goods by land to Lechlade or Cricklade, and then onward by the Thames; but their flocks doubtless could travel by Bath and go along the down ways eastward. But he says that now the roads are good, and mutton comes straight from the country in December, and almost as cheap as in summer.

I have not had the fortune to meet drovers from Wales, but where the Icknield Way through Buckinghamshire rounds the promontory Beacon of the Ivinghoe Hills I have seen men with sheep from Berkshire or Dorset journeying towards Dunstable, Royston, and the farms of Cambridgeshire and Suffolk. They have to go much on the hard grit to-day, and I have heard that they are kept off the unfenced Ridgeway lest the flock should eat too much of the pastures in their passage. The sheep dislike the grit as much as Mr. Burroughs loves it and I hate it, and what with the traffic and the harshness of the road it is not surprising to hear of a Welsh flock taking a week to get from Warminster to Monckton Deverill.

Where the high down roads are fenced there could be no better wayfaring. The track is twenty or thirty yards wide or more. It is untouched by wheels, and grows nothing but grass and the most delicate flowers. Along similar droves doubtless the sheep go up to the alpine grass in summer, as the shepherd in California told Miss Mary Austin.[1] "We went between the fenced pastures, feeding every other day and driving at night. In the dark we heard the bells ahead and slept upon our feet. Myself and another herdboy, we tied ourselves together not to wander from the road. . . . Whenever shepherds from the Rhone are met about camps in the Sierras they will be talking of how they slept upon their feet and followed after the bells." The best time to meet travelling sheep is after one of the fortnightly markets at East Ilsley among the Berkshire Downs, or at the time of the Ram Fair there on August 1st, or at the time of Tan Hill Fair on August 6th, or Yarnbury Fair on October 4th. Tan Hill and Yarnbury fairs are both held within the circuit of an old camp on the high chalk. Yarnbury is a meeting-place of trackways over Salisbury Plain. Tan Hill is close to the great Ridgeway and other trackways. Tan is supposed by some to be connected with the Celtic

[1] *The Flock*, by Mary Austin.

"tan," meaning fire, and with Celtic religious festivals having ceremonies of fire. This fair was held at a very early hour, and there is an obvious temptation to suggest a religious origin for the beacons said to have been lighted to guide the drovers.[1] I do not know what number of sheep would be sold at this fair. Defoe says that as many as five hundred thousand were sold at Weyhill Fair, one farmer attending to represent ten or twenty in his own county of Sussex or Oxfordshire. If this number came to Tan Hill it was worth a night's drenching to see the beacons and the multitudes arriving, to hear the bells and the sea of tired bleating and the sharp chiding of the overstrung dogs and the curses of the sleepy drovers upon that smooth, bare mountain without house or hut or a white road, or anything much newer than Wansdyke except the square of mustard that began to dawn through the mist like a banner not far away.

The Arab's answer to Mr. Doughty's[2] question whether he knew all the strange spires, pinnacles, and battlements of the wind-worn sand rock in the desert was that he knew "as good as every great stone" in all his marches over three or four thousand square miles; and there were drovers who could have said as much of the landmarks on the downs, the tumulus and camp, the furze thicket, the hawthorns, solitary or in line, the beech or fir clump, the church tower, the distant white wall

[1] *Wiltshire Archæological Magazine*, XXXIV.

[2] *Travels in Arabia*, by Charles M. Doughty.

or scallop of a chalk-pit, the white horse carved through the turf into the chalk, the church towers of the valley, the long coombes.

Even when deserted, these old roads are kept in memory by many signs. The grass refuses to grow over the still stream of turf in the same way as at either side of it. A line of thorn trees follows their course, or the hedge or fence or wall dividing two fields. They survive commonly and conspicuously as boundaries between fields, between estates, parishes, hundreds, and counties. It is one of the adventurous pleasures of a good map thus to trace the possible course of a known old road or to discover one that was lost. A distinct chain of footpath, lane, and road—road, lane, and footpath—leading across the country and corresponding in much of its course with boundaries is likely to be an ancient way. By this means much of the line of a road like the Icknield Way might be recovered if document and tradition had not preserved it. Without these signs few men to-day could tell an old from a new road, though, in fact, there are not many great lengths of entirely new road except in new towns and newly drained regions ; elsewhere the new roads have been made by linking up or improving old ones. The life of cities has destroyed at once the necessity and the power to judge the expanse of earth under our eyes, and few but soldiers educate whatever gift they have for this kind of judgment. If we learn to use a map, it is without fundamental understanding, without the savage's or the soldier's or the traveller's grasp ;

we must have inherited glimmerings of the old power, but they help us chiefly to an æsthetic appreciation of landscape. Let a man take an old map—not a very old one, which may be faulty or deficient—of his own district, and see if he can really grasp the system of the hills and rivers, and the bones of the land and the essential roads, and not be long baffled merely by the absence of certain new roads and familiar names; for few old ones will have entirely disappeared. If he is not so baffled he has cause for pride. Many are to be found who can hardly read a map when going from north to south, i.e. down the map instead of up it, with the east on the left and the west on the right and the north behind; and their difficulty is increased by being in a railway train. Such men may be very good walkers and very good men, though they be walking for exercise, or to improve body or soul, which is a reason that has lately been condemned by Mr. Belloc. "The detestable habit of walking for exercise," he tells us, "warps the soul."[1] He is perhaps assuming that the man always keeps this one object in view, and is always looking at his watch or feeling his pulse. But even a man walking for exercise may forget his object and unexpectedly profit; he may surprise happiness by the wayside or beyond the third stile, and no man can do more, whether he have the best and the most Bellocian object in the world. Then he condemns also men who ride along the road and

[1] See his Introduction to *The Footpath Way: an Anthology for Walkers.*

into an inn yard and feel that they are " like some one in a book." This is a rather serious matter. Authors have unintentionally persuaded simple men to suffer many blisters for the chance of drinking ale in the manner of Borrow and meeting adventures, in the hope of being heartily and Whitmanesquely democratic. Even Leslie Stephen half-seriously lamented that he was unworthy of Borrovian adventures ; for they never fell to him. A writer in the *Gentleman's Magazine* has made a good piece of prose in which he speaks of himself reading the *Essays of Elia* in an old inn at Llandovery—as Hazlitt read *La Nouvelle Heloise* at Llangollen on his birthday. A great many must be walking over England nowadays for the primary object of writing books : it has not been decided whether this is a worthy object. Mr. John Burroughs also condemns a walk taken as a prescription, but goes so far as to regard walking itself as a virtue. He says that his countrymen " have fallen from that state of grace which capacity to enjoy a walk implies " ; that they pride themselves on small feet, though " a little foot never yet supported a great character." He says they could " walk away from all their ennui, their worldly cares, their uncharitableness, their pride of dress ; for these devils always want to ride, while the simple virtues are never so happy as on foot." He concludes by singing " the sweetness of gravel and good sharp quartz-grit." He must be singing the grit of yester-year, or he never walked all day in the full blaze of summer upon the grit between

Newmarket and Hitchin. Leslie Stephen thought the true walker one to whom walking " is in itself delightful " ; he regarded walking as a panacea for authors, and believed that it could have cured Johnson and made Byron like Scott. A year or

The Icknield Way and Old Parallel Tracks, near Newmarket.

two ago Mr. Harold Munro took a month across France into Italy, for a part of the time putting himself out of reach of letters—to prove to himself that he could do it. There are plenty of adventures in modern life, but we still crave for the conspicuous ones which look so splendid when their heroes are distant or in the grave. These are the only adventures which we deign to recognize as such, and walking being a primitive act "natural to man," as Mr. Belloc says, we feel restored to a pristine majesty, or Arcadianism at least, when we undertake it. Perhaps if we walk long enough we shall discover something about roads. There could be few better objects for walking, unless it be to meet a mistress or to fetch a doctor. We walk for a thousand reasons, because we are tired of sitting, because we cannot rest, to get away from towns or to get into them, or because we cannot afford to ride; and for permanent use the last is perhaps the best, as it is the oldest.

CHAPTER II

HISTORY, MYTH, TRADITION, CONJECTURE, AND INVENTION

FEW in the multitude of us who now handle maps are without some vague awe at the Old English lettering of the names of ancient things, such as Merry Maidens, Idlebush Barrow, Crugian Ladies, or the plain Carn, Long Barrow, or Dolmen. Not many could explain altogether why these are impressive. We remember the same lettering in old mysterious books, and in Scott's *Marmion* and Wordsworth's *Hartleap Well.* We are touched in our sense of unmeasured antiquity, we acknowledge the honour and the darkness of the human inheritance. Most impressive of all, because they recur across many counties, are the names of roads, like the Sarn Helen of Wales, the Pilgrims' Way of England. It is part of their power that they have no obvious and limited significance, and were certainly not bestowed by king or minister as names are given by a merchant to his commodities. Instead of "London Road" we see "Watling Street"; instead of "North Road" there is "Foss Way" or "Ermine Street." But all these make some appeal, however fantastical, to the intelligence.

"Icknield Street" or "Icknield Way" makes no such appeal. It is the name of two apparently distinct roads: one with a Roman look running north and south through Worcestershire and Warwickshire, the other winding with the chalk hills through Suffolk, Cambridgeshire, Hertfordshire, Bedfordshire, Buckinghamshire, Oxfordshire, Berkshire, and Wiltshire. I shall confine myself as far as possible to this second road. It runs south-westwards from East Anglia and along the Chilterns to the Downs and Wessex; but the name is mysterious. For centuries—since Holinshed—it was supposed to be connected with the East Anglian kingdom of the Iceni: only fifty years ago Guest confidently translated it as the warpath of the Iceni, and connected it with the names of places along its course, such as Icklingham, Ickleton, and Ickleford. To-day, it is pointed out with equal confidence that "according to philological laws Iceni would have produced in England a form beginning with Itch- or Etch-." Dr. Henry Bradley cannot believe that there was any knowledge of the Iceni in Berkshire, but finds it "a natural supposition" that the road was called after a woman named Icenhild, though he points out that no such person or name is known in myth or history.

It is a pleasure to see a learned man of the twentieth century thus playing at the invention of a twilight deity as the patroness of an old road, like the Helen or Elen of Wales. Two hundred years ago his invention would have been wholly serious and generations of equally serious and less inventive

D

antiquaries would have followed him. There have been other explanations. Camden, at the same time as Holinshed, accepted the connection with the Iceni, but "what the origin of the name should be," he says in his *Suffolk*, "as God shall help me, I dare not guess, unless one should derive it from the *wedgy* figure of the county, and refer to its lying upon the ocean in form of a *wedge*. For the Britons in their language call a wedge Iken. . . ." John Aubrey had it from "Mr. Meredith Lloyd" that "Ychen is upper, as to say the upper country or people," and that "Ychen" also signifies "oxen." Wise, in 1738, linked it with the name of Agricola, because of the significant core of Ick, or in the form "Ryknield," rick. Willis, in 1787, said that the road took its name from the Itchen, believing that it began at Southampton and went parallel to that river to Winchester; and that Iken-eld was the Saxon name for the Old Iken Street. The poet William Barnes, lover of ancient Britons, said that it might come from a word meaning high or upper, either because it was "an upcast way" or because it was the "upper or eastern road," while Ryknield seemed to him to come from a word meaning a trench, and therefore a "hollow way." And still nobody knows or believes that anybody else knows. The name, therefore, throws no light at present on the use or history of the road.

Much has been written about the Icknield Way by antiquaries from the sixteenth to the nineteenth centuries. Most of them regarded the road as one of the four royal roads or Roman roads of Britain, on the authority not of local evidence and direct examination, but of half-mythic laws and histories. The earliest of these are "The Laws of Edward the Confessor." Here four roads are mentioned—Watlinge strete, Fosse, Hikenilde strete, and Erminge strete—two of them extending across the breadth of the land and two throughout the length; and travellers on them were protected by the king's peace. But Liebermann assigns as a probable date to these laws a year between 1130 and 1135: Pollock and Maitland, in their *History of English Law*, condemn the work as a compilation of the last years of Henry I; having something of the nature of a political pamphlet and being adorned with pious legends, "its statements, when not supported by other evidence, will hardly tell us more than that sane men of the twelfth century would have liked these statements to be true." The French version of the "Laws of William the Conqueror" is almost word for word the same as the Laws of the Confessor in the matter of the royal roads: the Latin version omits Hykenild strete. Roger de Hoveden, in 1200, uses almost the same words: so does Henry of Huntingdon in 1130, except that he describes the Icknield Way as going out of the east into the west.

Mr. Harold Peake suggests to me that these writers may all have had as their inspiration the brilliant Geoffrey of Monmouth, who wrote the *History of the British Kings* in the early twelfth century. He tells us, in language not more credible than that of "The Dream of Maxen" in the *Mabinogion*, that

King Belinus commanded four roads to be made over the length and breadth of the island :—

"Especially careful was he [King Belinus] to proclaim that the cities and the highways that led unto the city should have the same peace that Dunwallo had established therein. But dissension arose as concerning the highways, for that none knew the line whereby their boundaries were determined. The king therefore, being minded to leave no loophole for quibbles in the law, called together all the workmen of the whole island, and commanded a highway to be builded of stone and mortar that should cut through the entire length of the island from the Cornish sea to the coast of Caithness, and should run in a straight line from one city unto another the whole of the way along. A second also he bade be made across the width of the kingdom, which, stretching from the city of Menevia on the sea of Demetia as far as Hamo's port, should show clear guidance to the cities along the line. Two others also he made to be laid out slantwise athwart the island so as to afford access unto the other cities. Then he dedicated them with all honour and dignity, and proclaimed it as of his common law, that condign punishment should be inflicted on any that should do violence to other thereon. But if any would fain know all of his ordinances as concerning them, let him read the Molmutine laws that Gildas the historian did translate out of the British into Latin, and King Alfred out of the Latin into the English tongue."

This great north-and-south road is like Ermine

Street, the slantwise roads might be Watling Street and the Foss Way, and that across the width from Menevia to "Hamo's port," the Icknield Way. As Geoffrey makes one road go from the Cornish sea to Caithness, so Henry of Huntingdon takes his Fosse Way from Totnes to Caithness. Henry, as is known, had read part or all of Geoffrey's book before it was given to the world and made an abstract of it; and the romancer had warned him to be silent as to the British kings, because he had not that book in the British tongue, brought from Brittany by Walter, Archdeacon of Oxford, and translated into Latin by Geoffrey himself. Here, as usual, it can safely be said that Geoffrey's words are not pure invention; but what his authority in writing or tradition may have been appears to be undiscoverable. He may have used some tradition which was the basis also of the account of the Empress Helen's road-making in "The Dream of Maxen." He may have used the so-called laws of Dynwal Moel Mud —"before the crown of London and the supremacy of this island were seized by the Saxons"—who measured the length and breadth of the island, in order "to know its journeys by days." (*Laws and Institutes of Wales: Vendotian Code.*) Henry of Huntingdon may well have been a meek adapter of Geoffrey's majestic statements, and some local knowledge of his own may have helped him to put names upon the roads of Belinus. To this second road from St. David's (Menevia) to Hamo's port or Southampton he gives the name of Ichenild or Ikenild. Walter Map, in *De Nugis Curialium* (*circa* 1188), speaks of Canute holding London and the land beyond Hickenild, and Edmund the rest; the Anglo-Saxon *Chronicle* says that Edmund had Wessex and Canute the "north part" or Mercia; and these two together help to define the road.

Whether Henry of Huntingdon's history owed anything to Geoffrey, Robert of Gloucester's metrical chronicle (*circa* 1300) certainly did, for he refers to Belinus as the road-maker; but, like Henry, he calls the road from Totnes to Caithness the Fosse. Of the Icknield Street he says that it went from east to west, and also, apparently, that it was the road from St. David's to Southampton through Worcester, Cirencester, and Winchester. A writer of *circa* 1360, Ralph Higden, mentions Belin, and he gives two theories about the Fosse, but evidently himself knows nothing. He calls the east-and-west road from St. David's to Southampton Watling Street. His fourth road goes from south to north, from St. David's, by Worcester and Birmingham, Lichfield and Derby, Chesterfield and York, to Tynemouth; and its name varies in different manuscripts from Rikenildstrete to Hikenilstrete. Guest has pointed out that Higden was following Geoffrey. In the *Eulogium Historiarum* (1362) this road goes from south to north from St. David's to Tynemouth, and is called once Belinstrete, and three times Hykeneldstret or Hikeneldstret. The author does not mention Ermine Street, but two Belinstretes, the other going from St. David's to Southampton. It is likely that none of these men except Geoffrey and perhaps Henry could have mapped the roads.

The one map of the period showing the roads is such as they might have been expected to make. It belongs probably to the thirteenth century and was reproduced by Hearne, from a British Museum manuscript, in Vol. V of his edition of Leland's *Itinerary* (1710). It shows the four roads by means of lines and a brief description—his Fosse going in the approved manner from Totnes to Caithness, the Ermine Street due north and south, the Watling Street from south-east to north-west. Ykenild Street goes straight across from west to east. The artist's description of this as of the other roads is almost word for word from Henry of Huntingdon. But there are these differences and additions: the western extremity of the Icknield Way is not called St. David's, but Salisbury, which is thus placed due north of Totnes where St. David's should be; the eastern—or, as he calls it, the southern—is St. Edmunds. At the point of intersection with Watling Street he writes "Dunstaple," which is accurate. Thus he is original only in his description of the Icknield Way. In putting "Meridies" by St. Edmunds he made a slip due to his drawing the map with its north end on the right side. It is impossible to decide the extent of his mistake in marking Salisbury at the west end of the road. He may have believed that it went to Salisbury, but have been afraid to deviate from the received opinion that it was an east-and-west road; or he may simply have put Salisbury in mistake for St. David's. Giving Bury St. Edmunds as the eastern termination suggests local knowledge which the accurate position of Dunstable confirms. He may have been a man of the eastern counties who thought that Salisbury was not only the end of the road, as travellers told him, but a city in the west.

Holinshed, in his *Chronicles* (1586), mentions Geoffrey as the authority for the origin of the four great roads, and, after quoting him, goes on to describe an "Ikenild or Rikenild" beginning somewhere in the south and going through Worcester, Birmingham, and Chesterfield to the mouth of the Tyne. "I take it," he says, "to be called the Ikenild, because it passed through the kingdome of the Icenes. For albeit that Leland and others following him doo seeme to place the Icenes in Norffolke and Suffolke; yet in mine opinion that cannot well be doone, sith it is manifest by Tacitus that they laie neere unto the Silures, and (as I gesse) either in Stafford and Worcester shires, or in both, except my conjecture doo fail me." Here it is to be noticed, first, that he gives Ikenild and Rikenild as alternative names of one road and, second, that he sees the resemblance between "Ikenild" and "Iceni." He has evidently thought about the matter, but he shows no trace of local knowledge or curiosity. Camden (1586) also only mentions the road in his introduction to the subject of the Iceni; though he has to speak of many places touched by the road, he ignores the fact, if he ever knew it. The poet Drayton, in his *Polyolbion* (1616), substitutes "Michael's utmost Mount" for Totnes at the south end of the Fosse Way, and takes Watling Street from Dover to "the farth'st of fruitful Anglesey," and he writes like a Warwickshire man of the country where those two roads cross (Song xiii, 11, 311 *et seq.;* Song xxvi, 11, 43 *et seq.*). In the "Sixteenth Song" of *Polyolbion* he makes Watling sing of herself and her "three sister streets":—

Since us, his kingly ways, Mulmutius first began,
From sea again to sea, that through the Island ran.
Which that in mind to keep posterity might have,
Appointing first our course, this privilege he gave,
That no man might arrest, or debtors' goods might seize
In any of us four his military ways.

Having sung of the Fosse, Watling continues:—

But O, unhappy chance! through time's disastrous lot,
Our other fellow streets lie utterly forgot:
As Icning, that set out from Yarmouth in the East,
By the Iceni then being generally possest,
Was of that people first term'd Icning in her race,
Upon the Chiltern here that did my course imbrace:
Into the dropping South, and bearing then outright,
Upon the Solent Sea stopt on the Isle-of-Wight.

"Rickneld" he takes from St. David's to Tynemouth.

It is very clear that Drayton had read Geoffrey or a disciple. The notes to *Polyolbion* reveal the fact that Selden accepted Molmutius and his laws. "Take it upon credit of the British story" are his words. He accepted also King Belin and the making of the four roads; but having noticed that authorities vary as to their courses and even their names, he is content to say, "To endeavour certainty in them were but to obtrude unwarrantable conjecture, and abuse time and you." Evidently he knew these roads as a whole neither from personal knowledge nor from contemporary report, but only from books. Had he known anything he would have betrayed it, for he digresses to tell the little that he knows of "Stanstreet in Surrey."

Drayton apparently knew more, though perhaps all his knowledge was not available for verse. He is the first to distinguish clearly between the Ricknield and the Icknield Street. He takes the Icknield Way from Yarmouth to the Solent; the definite "Yarmouth," now for the first time connected with the road, the use of the variant Icning, the connection with the Chilterns, the crossing of Watling Street—all suggest local knowledge. Here more than ever it is to be wished that Drayton had either written his book in prose or had given his authorities and his actual notes of local lore. He was a great lover of England and of Wales, and could have written one of the finest prose books of the seventeenth century had he put down what he knew without ramming it into the mould of rhyme.

Of all these men except Drayton and the man who drew the map, none betrays personal knowledge of the road. They are all writing of something either too generally known to need explanation or of something which they know only from other writers. All their words together hardly do more than prove that there was or had formerly been a road, known as Ricknield or Icknield Street; or at most that there were or had been three roads bearing those names—one from St. David's east and then north to Tynemouth; a second running southwestwards across the east of England from

Norfolk to Southampton; and a third from St. David's to Southampton. The second seems to owe nothing to Geoffrey, and all the local knowledge, such as it is, is so far connected with this.

In 1677 appeared a book by one who had not only heard of the four royal roads, but had met with what he believed to be one of them. This was Robert Plot's *Natural History of Oxfordshire.* He says:—

"Of the four Basilical, Consular, or Prætorian ways, or Chemini majores, I have met with but one that passeth through this County, the discovery whereof yet I hope may prove acceptable, because not described before, or its footsteps any where noted by Sir H. Spelman, Mr. Camden, or any other Author that I have read or could hear of: whereat indeed I cannot but very much wonder, since it is called by its old name at very many places [Ikenildway] to this very day. Some indeed call it Icknil, some Acknil, others Hackney, and some again Hackington, but all intend the very same way, that stretches it self in this County from North-east to South-west; coming into it (out of Bucks) at the Parish of Chinner, and going out again over the Thames (into Berks) at the Parish of Goreing. The reason, I suppose, why this way was not raised, is, because it lies along under the Chiltern Hills on a firm fast ground, having the hills themselves as a sufficient direction: which is all worth notice of it, but that it passes through no town or village in the County, but only Goreing; nor does it (as I hear) scarce any where else, for which reason 'tis much used by stealers of Cattle: and secondly, that it seems by its pointing to come from Norfolk and Suffolk, formerly the Kingdom of the Iceni, from whom most agree (and perhaps rightly enough) it received its name Icenild or Ikenild; and to tend the other way westward perhaps into Devonshire and Cornwall, to the Land's End."

He adds, with some triumph, that Holinshed was much mistaken, but he suspends his judgment because he has read in Dugdale's *Antiquities of Warwickshire* of an "Ickle-street" in that county. He prints a map showing the road passing, all on its right hand as it goes south, the villages of "Kempton," Chinner, Oakley, Crowell Kingston, Aston Rowant, Lewkner, Sherborne, Watlington, the Britwells, Ewelme, Croamish Gifford, Nuneham, Warren, Mungewell, the three Stokes, and then south of Goring Church. He adds that under "Stokenchurch Hills," about Lewkner and Aston Rowant, there are two Icknield ways, an upper and a lower; and here it may be mentioned that Hearne's diary for September 29th, 1722, has the entry:—

"I went thro' Ewelm, a ¼ of a mile from which is Gouldsheath, and about 2 furlongs east said Ewelm passeth the *lower Hackneyway*."

Plot gives a substance to a name. He proves the existence of a road bearing the name of Icknield and variations of it, and having a course along the Chilterns, like Drayton's road. He does not exaggerate; in fact, he thinks it a poor sort of road when compared with the Icknield Street through Staffordshire, of which he says :—

"I look upon this of Staffordshire as the most remarkable of the two, and so to be that Iknild street, which is usually reckoned to be one of the four basilical or great ways of England, and not that of Oxfordshire, this being raised all along and paved at some places, and very signal almost wherever it goes, whereas that of Oxfordshire is not so there, whatever it may be in other counties."

The next evidence is eighteen years later, and comes from the maps by Robert Morden illustrating Gibson's edition of Camden's *Britannia* (1695). His map of Hertfordshire suddenly introduces us to a road called the Icknal or Icnal Way, running west from Royston—perhaps even from Barley, three miles south-east of Royston—through Baldock, then more and more south-east, over the Lea to the north of Luton, through Dunstable, and so, leaving on its right hand Toternhoe, Edlesborough, Ivinghoe, and Marsworth, going out of the map with Wilston on its right. In the map of Buckinghamshire this road is continued through Wendover, and passes Princes Risborough and Bledlow. In the map of Oxfordshire it is called "Icknield Way," and follows a line like that in Plot's map, crossing "Grime's Dike," leaving Ipsden and Woodcot on its left, reaching the Thames on the south of Goring Church. The Berkshire map does not show any road of this or similar name, or any one corresponding to it. Nor is the road to be found on the maps of Essex, Cambridgeshire, Suffolk, or Norfolk. The extension of it through Buckinghamshire and Hertfordshire may well have come from the local knowledge of Morden or a collaborator. There must have been abundant information of the kind used by Plot which escaped antiquaries who were thinking about a royal road, a majestic basilical or consular way, running from St. David's to Southampton, or farther. John Aubrey (died 1697), the man to tap this local lore, had nothing to say of any such road in his own county of Wiltshire, but he left some rough notes. He connects "Iceni" with "Ikenild," and remarks (on the authority of Wren) that there were three Itchings on Ikenel Street, including Itching Stoke in Hampshire, where the Pilgrims' Way fords the Itchen. He says also that a Mr. Sherwood told him of "an Ikenil way from North Yarmouth to Plymouth; the country people will say, 'Keep along the Ikenil Way,' *scilicet* the Wallington Hills." Wallington is two miles south-east of Baldock and south of the Icknield Way, and through it ran a parallel road (mentioned in *Archæological Journal*, Vol. XXV) from Barley, by Therfield, Strethall, Sandon, and Wallington to Clothall; but the term "Wallington Hills" does not exclude the Icnal Way marked in Morden's map. The precise *North* Yarmouth may also have been accurate, and I should be inclined to believe that at that day men sometimes went between Plymouth and North Yarmouth by a road or chain of roads known through perhaps a very large part of its course by some such name as Ikenil Way.

A period of antiquarian conjecture and invention was now beginning, with exploration often of an active kind, but usually kept sternly in obedience to speculation. At the end of the sixth volume of Hearne's *Leland* (1710) is an essay supposed to be by Roger Gale (1672–1744). He has no doubt about "four great roads," but regards the story of Molmutius and Belinus as exploded, and says that "nobody now questions but that" the Romans made them. He distinguishes, "as does Mr. Drayton," between Icknield and Ricknield, and complains of the old confusion. The Icknield Way, "which has its rise and name from the people called Iceni," he finds first "with any certainty near Barley in Herts," as in Robert Morden's map; but he suggests an eastern continuation through Ickleton, "and so by Gogmagog hills, and over Newmarket Heath to Ikesworth, not two miles south from St. Edmundsbury," and possibly to Burgh Castle, near Yarmouth. Returning westward, he describes a course which might have been taken from Morden's map, except that in the neighbourhood of Luton it touches Streatley instead of Leagrave, and goes to Houghton Regis as well as to Dunstable. But having reached Buckinghamshire, he cannot find it "anywhere apparent to the eye . . . except between Princes Risborrow and Kemble in the Street, where it is still call'd Icknell Way." These are words which suggest that the eye was not his own. In Oxfordshire he leaves the road to Plot. At Goring and Streatley he does not know what to do, because his guides—Henry of Huntingdon and Drayton and others—disagree. He conjectures a continuation to Southampton, another through Speen to Salisbury and beyond, where he has found the name "Aggleton Road," locally given to the road near Badbury Castle, the Roman road from Old Sarum to Dorchester. He thinks "Aggleton Road" can have no connection with Ickleton, but he shows no other reason for believing that his Roman road is the Icknield Way.

In 1724 appeared the *Itinerarium Curiosum* of Gale's friend William Stukeley (1687–1765), M.D., F.R.S., F.R.C.P. Here he describes an exploration of the Icknield Way. He takes it through Ickleton and, like Gale, through Streatley, near Luton; he mentions the lovely prospect from the northern sides of the Chilterns and a few more place-names. East of Ickleton, or his newly discovered Roman camp at Great Chesterford, he speaks of the road going along the boundary between Essex and Cambridgeshire "towards Icleworth in Suffolk." He thinks the road Roman. Beyond the Thames he has no uncertainty like Gale. He says straight out that at Speen "the great Icening-street road coming from the Thames at Goring . . . crosses the Kennet river"; also that he found it a little north of Bridport going to Dorchester, and accompanied it "with no small pleasure." If he had any reason for calling any part of this road "the great Icening Street of the Romans," it has never been discovered, nor has anything else confirmed his view, except that Leland saw two Roman milestones between Streatley and Aldworth, which have been seen since, but never described except in rumour. William Stukeley, M.D., F.R.S., F.R.C.P., who read "Oriuna" for "Fortuna" on a coin, and so invented the belief that one Oriuna was the wife of Carausius, was soon afterwards unanswerably questioned and plainly contradicted on matters of fact by Smart Lethieullier (1701–60) and Richard Willis. He is chiefly memorable here because the now venerable title of *Via Iceniana* was conferred by him on the road which he chose to believe the Icknield Way. The title, translated back into Icknield Street, is still generally accepted.

Francis Wise (1697–1767) found the road where Gale had lost it, beyond the ford at Streatley. In his book on *Some Antiquities in Berkshire* he says that it loses its name at Streatley, but is "visible enough" to Blewbury and known as the Great Reading Road. From Blewbury through Upton and Harwell this road is called the Portway, yet he thinks that it may be the Icknield Way notwithstanding; or, if not, there is an alternative to the south, lost in the ploughland until near Lockinge it becomes a raised way called "Icleton Meer"; while after Wantage it is the "Ickleton Way," going "all under the hills between them and Childrey," Sparsholt, Uffington, so under White-horse-hill, leaving Woolston and Compton on the right, thence to Ashbury and Bishopstone. He thought that it was making rather for Avebury than for Salisbury. This road is marked as Eccleton Street in Roque's fine eighteenth-century map of Berkshire, though it is not easy to be certain of the road indicated by the name, except that it runs at the foot of the hills.

Richard Willis, in an essay posthumously published in *Archæologia*, VIII (1787), claims to be the discoverer of two Roman roads which "fortunately" crossed one another near his house at Andover. One of these was the road from Southampton by Winchester and Cirencester to Gloucester, and this was, he says, "I doubt not the Ikeneld Street." He does not say why he is certain, but his authority or inspiration was probably Geoffrey or a disciple. He had an eye for old roads, but too generally honoured them with the name of Roman. He noticed the old road leaving his supposed Icknield Street on the right a mile south of Ogbourne St. George, and going north-east to the inn now called "The Shepherd's Rest" at Totterdown, which is on the Roman road from Speen to Cirencester. Among several roads connecting this Roman "Icknield Street" with the Ermine Street he mentions a road which he calls a causeway, from Royston to Ogbourne St. George, or at least to Bishopston and Wanborough. This has been called Icknield Street, but he will call it the "Oxford Icknield Street," which, he says, from coinciding with his real Icknield Street at Wanborough, acquired its name. It would be as reasonable to say that London took its name from the London County Council, or that Julius Cæsar took his from Julius Cæsar Scaliger. The unquestionable fact—known to him from Morden's map, from Plot, and from Wise—that there is a road with the name of Icknield Way, or a variant of it, between Royston and Wanborough, he regards as a "stumbling block," because it stands in the way of theorists less insolent than himself.

Lysons' *Magna Britannia* (1806) brings together two more such opposites as Wise and Willis. In "Berkshire" a letter is quoted from a Mr. Church, surveyor of Wantage, describing the Berkshire road, where Wise had been uncertain, in its eastern half. Mr. Church writes:—

"The Ickleton-way has been ploughed up across Wantage East Field till it enters Charlton (a hamlet of Wantage); it then passes through West Lockinge. It is lost across Mr. Bastard's park in East Lockinge, but appears again from that park to Ginge Brook, in Ardington parish. It passes by White's barn in Sparsholt-court manor, and is afterwards ploughed up for some way, but appears again, after crossing the Newbury-way, by Wiltshire's and Halve-hill barns, in East Hendred parish; from thence through the parishes of Harwell, West Hagbourne, and the hamlet of Upton, to the village of Blewbury, and through the parishes of Aston Tirrold, and Cholsey, to Moulsford on the Thames, and thence to Streatley; from Upton to Streatley it forms part of the new turnpike road from Wantage to Reading." From Upton station to the east edge of Lockinge Park this road is now an almost continuous series of cart-tracks known—at least, in the neighbourhood of East Hendred, which it leaves half a mile to the north—as Ickleton Street or Ickleton Meer. This evidence of 1911,

"Ickleton Meer," Hagbourne Hill, near Upton, Berks.

confirming statements made a hundred and two hundred years ago, is sufficient to identify that portion of the road as Ickleton Street. Beyond Wantage, Wise's description can be applied only to the modern road from Wantage to Bishopston, or as far as the "Calley Arms" at Wanborough. East of Upton the modern road to Streatley—the old Reading turnpike—has a rival in a series of cart-tracks through Blewbury and the Astons, and possibly to be connected with the "Papist Way" near Cholsey.

Thus there is traditional authority for giving the name of Ickleton Street or Way to a series of roads in Berkshire between Bishopston and Streatley, and the name of Icknield or Icnal Way to a road leading from Royston to Goring; and hence a probability that the two were united by the ford between Streatley and Goring. To this can be added a strong impression that this road came from a Norfolk port and went westward to Avebury, and thence or by another route into Devon or Cornwall; but not one writer, except perhaps Aubrey's friend, proves or even implies a contemporary use of this road throughout its course; while Drayton and Plot suggest that it had fallen into decay in their time.

Along with "Mr. Church, surveyor of Wantage," in Lysons' *Berkshire*, appeared a bishop, John Bennet (1746–1820), Bishop of Cloyne from 1794 until his death. Without any argument or evidence he makes the following pronouncement, heralded by the editorial opinion that "his researches have enabled him to speak with certainty on the subject" :—

"The Ikeneld enters Berkshire from Oxfordshire at Streatley, where it seems to have divided: one branch by the name of the Ridgeway continued on the edge of the high ground by Cuckhamsley and White-horse-hill into Wiltshire; pointing, as Mr. Wise observes, rather to Avebury or the Devizes than Salisbury; while the other branch went from Streatley, perhaps by Hampstead and Hermitage, under the name of the West Ridge, to Newbury, and thence it may be to Old Sarum."

At first he seems to misunderstand Wise, and to suppose that his Ickleton Street was a road on the unpopulated ridge and not in the valley past a string of villages, and he goes on afterwards to assert that this valley road is Roman and seems to come from a spot near or rather below Wallingford. In 1806 the Rev. Henry Beeke (*Archæologia*, XV) expressed the opinion that the Icknield Way crossed the Thames at Moulsford. As Bennet gives no reason he makes no apology. His reason for giving the name of West Ridge to a road running *east* of its fellow must have been that it went through the village of Westridge, where doubtless the road was called the Westridge Way, as the road from Chevington is called the Chevington Way, and so on. He had apparently no reason for choosing the Ridgeway except that it came from the same ford at Streatley reached by the Icknield Way at Goring. Nevertheless, he has been so persistently followed that the Ridgeway is now given by the Ordnance

Survey the alternative title of "Icknield Way," and also of "Roman Road," which even the bishop said it was not; some Berkshire people even call the Ridgeway the Icknield Way because it is the "Government name"; and "West Ridge Way" is attached with all the honour of Old English lettering to the more easterly road. Bennet equals Stukeley in the grandeur of his fiction and the veneration which it has earned. In Lysons' *Cambridgeshire* (1808) he takes the road through Newmarket, herein coinciding with later-proved facts, but continues it to Ickleton on the east of the modern turnpike along a course never yet identified.

Men who were not bishops now begin to exercise themselves in suggesting roads which may have been continuations of this Ickleton or Icknield Way. They print their opinions with varying degrees of certainty. In 1829 Dr. Mason, rector of Orford, in Suffolk (*Archæologia*, XXIII), traces it, "after it leaves Ixworth," to Buckenham and thence by two forks to Caistor and to Burgh Castle. Samuel Woodward, in 1830 (*Archæologia*, XXIII), also assumes that it passes through Buckenham, Ixworth, and Bury St. Edmunds. In 1833 Alfred John Kempe (*Archæologia*, XXVI) takes it for granted that the road "crossed the kingdom from Norwich towards Old Sarum." With an "I need hardly observe," he connects the road with the Iceni, and explains it as "the Iken-eld-strete, that is, the old street or way of the Iceni." Arthur Taylor (*Archæological Institute: Memoirs*, 1847; Norwich volume) connects the road with Norwich Castle Hill, which he believes to be British. Like the Ordnance Survey map, he takes it through Newmarket, Kentford, Cavenham, Lackford, and Thetford. Like Bennet, both Woodward and Taylor regard the road as a British trackway. But Taylor earns his chief distinction by the possession of a deed "apparently of the reign of Henry iii," relating to premises at Newmarket and "extending upon Ykenildweie."

In 1856, in the form of a discourse afterwards embodied in his *Origines Celticæ* (1883), Edwin Guest wrote a long account of the Icknield Way. He mentions as evidence charters of the tenth century referring to estates in Berkshire between Blewbury and Wayland's Smithy, so minute, he says, as almost to be sufficient foundation for a map, but not to enable him to trace the road; for he accepts Bennet's substitution of the Ridgeway. North of the Thames his earliest evidence is a parchment, possibly of the fourteenth century, relating to the foundation of Dunstable Priory at a place where the two royal roads of Watling and Ickneld cross, a place of woods and robbers near Houghton. He quotes a "letter testimonial of 1476" proving that this trackway, west of Dunstable, was known as Ikeneld Strete. He takes the road from Icklingham and through Ickleton and Ickleford because that is a possible course and because he believes those names to be connected with "Iceni" and "Icknield." What was the one great road described as Icknield Street in the *Laws of the Confessor* he finds it hard to define. But he can find no traces of Roman construction in the road. Inspired by the map showing Salisbury at the end of the road, he suggests that "most probably" it joined the Ridgeway east of Avebury and continued along its course, as recently described by Sir Richard Colt Hoare.

Messrs. Woodward and Wilks, in their history of Hampshire (1861–9), are well acquainted with the many theories of the road, and "on the whole see most reason" for agreeing with Drayton, but also for giving the name to the Roman road from Winchester to Cirencester and Gloucester, or another Roman road running north-west of Basingstoke. They speak of the allegation that in ancient deeds the road to Gloucester is designated as Hicknel or Hicknal Way; but these have not been identified.

C. C. Babington, in his *Ancient Cambridgeshire* (1883), speaks of the road as easily traced from Thetford to Kentford, and he regards Woodward's British way from Norwich by Wymondham and Attleborough to Thetford as a continuation. But he has no documentary evidence, no tradition, and no local name to support his conjectures at any point between Norwich and Royston, except at Newmarket. He could not find Bennet's road from Newmarket east of the turnpike. Probably the bishop meant the roads west of Westley Waterless, past Linnet Hall, west of Weston Colville, West Wratting and Balsham; it is improbable that he did more than fly over them in fancy. He is satisfied that where the parish, and afterwards the county, boundaries coincide with the present road from Newmarket it is the Icknield Way, especially as at Stump Cross the county boundary follows the sudden turn out of the main road along a little-used lane leading over the Cam to Ickleton. From Ickleton to a point near Chrishall Grange and a tumulus—where for a mile the lane is a county boundary—it is uncertain; but from that point to Noon's Folly he is content with the "nearly disused track," which near there again becomes a county boundary. Thus he connects Newmarket and Royston by a road of the same character as the well-warranted parts of the Icknield Way without any evidence but probability.

The Rev. A. C. Yorke (*Proceedings of the Cambridge Antiquarian Society*, 1903) prefers the road known as Ashwell Street, which runs for some miles nearly parallel with the supposed Icknield Way and is most clear from Ashwell, north of Baldock, to Melbourn, north-east of Royston. In a lucid and vigorous article he says that "there can be no doubt" that "Ashwell Street is the original Icknield Way." He is willing to give up the name of one road, take away the name from another road which has borne it since 1695, and in one place since Henry the Third, and give it to the first which has never borne it, so far as he knows. He thinks the so-called Icknield Way from Newmarket to Hitchin, Roman; just as others think his Ashwell Street Roman, Mr. F. Codrington, e.g., holding that Ashwell Street was an alternative course, leaving the Icknield Way at Worsted Lodge and returning at Wilbury Camp.

Mr. W. G. Clarke (*Norwich Mercury*, Oct. 8, '04, etc.;

Knowledge, II, 99) attempts to connect Newmarket with Norwich and call the road the Icknield Way. He suggests a route over the Kennett at Kentford and the Lark at Lackford; then to Icklingham All Saints, and following the boundary of the hundreds of Blackbourn and Lackford to Thetford, having

Wilbury Camp.

crossed the road from Newmarket to Thetford at Marmansgrave, and that between Bury and Thetford a few yards north of Thetford Gasworks, where the remains of a British settlement were found in 1870. He crosses the Little Ouse and Thet where the Nuns' Bridges now are. On the other side "the logical and undoubtedly correct continuation of the Icknield Way" is by Castle Lane and Green Lane. A find of Celtic and Roman pottery at the south end of Green Lane, old thorns in the fields between Green Lane and Roudham Heath, old banks on the heath near Peddars' Way, " which it crosses about half a mile from where Peddars' Way is joined by the Drove," a " Bridgham tradition " of a waggon road over Roudham Heath, and the battle of Ringmore, fought there between Sweyn and Ulfketel, the find of bronze weapons and flint axes at Attleborough, and the supposed British origin of Norwich Castle Hill, take him by these places. From Norwich he goes by Sprowston, Rackheath, Wroxham, Hoveton, Beeston, over the Ant by the " Devil's Ditch," or " Roman Camp," at Wayford to Stalham and to Happisburgh. Except that Stalham is near Hickling, this route has nothing—no local map, no documents—to entitle it to be called the Icknield Way.

Mr. Beloe (Cambridge Antiquarian Society, *Proceedings*, VII) suggests an easterly line beyond Newmarket by a supposed junction with the Ailesway from Newmarket, by Brandon Ferry and Narford to Hunstanton.

Mr. J. C. Tingey (*Norfolk Archæology*, XIV) agrees that such a junction may have been used, but prefers a line through Ickburgh and Cockley Cley, crossing the Wissey at Mundford. He also proposes another route from Lackford almost to Thetford, which he avoids, crossing the Ouse on to Snarehill, with its many tumuli, because he thinks an early traveller would have done this. Then, with no trace of a road, he goes over Snare Hill to Shadwell Park, the Harlings, Uphall, Kenninghall to Banham, where a street was once called Tycknald Street (Blomefield's *History of Norfolk*); or he could reach Banham from Elvedon, Barnham, and Rushford. After Banham he leaves a gap of twelve miles, hastening to Swainsthorpe, south-east of Norwich, where he has found a Hickling Lane, called "Icklinge Way," in a seventeenth-century conveyance, where it is said to lead to Kenninghall. He has also found in Blomefield a mention of "the way called Ykenelds-gate," in that parish, dated 1308.

The partly lost line of this lane he has made out through Mulbarton; beyond which he is struck by the place-names of Keningham, Kentlow, and Kenninghall, noticing the other similar names on or near the supposed Icknield Way—Kentford, Kennet, Kensworth (once "Ikensworth"), Kennett, in Wiltshire, and, beyond Exeter, Kenn and Kenn Ford. Other documents of 1482 and 1658 relating to the next parish to Swainsthorpe, Stoke Holy Cross, enable him to extend the road with some probability eastward. They also show that the road was known at about the same time as Hickley Lane in one parish, and Stoke Long Lane in another. Most remarkable of all, he has found in Blomefield mention of "the way called Ykeneldsgate" in the same parish of Stoke Holy Cross, in 1306. He suggests reaching Haddiscoe as his "port in Celtic times," by Framingham Earl, Bergh Apton, Thurton Church, Loddon, and Raveningham. He sternly avoids Norwich as post-Roman, and Bury for the same reason. At the same time he admits the probability of branches to those places when they became important. Thus he shows that he has in his mind one road, with one name, and that something like Icknield Street, going from sea to sea, not only in the Confessor's time, but before the Romans.

It is impossible even to outline the multitudinous conjectures at the north-east end of the Icknield Way. At the south-west conjecture has been all but silenced by Stukeley's invention of the Via Iceniana and Bennet's substitution of the Ridgeway, both stupefying fictions.

For two hundred years these conjectures have been multiplied and become venerable by repetition. Plot thinks that the road might go from Norfolk to Devon and Land's End. Gale fancies Caistor and Burgh Castle at one end, and, as Stukeley did, Exeter at the other. Dr. Beeke "supposes" it went from Streatley towards Silchester, also that it crossed the Thames at Moulsford. Colt Hoare speaks of it as connecting Old Sarum with Dorchester and Winchester. Arthur Taylor takes it for granted that it came from "Cornwall or some extreme point in the south-west of Britain" to Norwich and Hickling. Isaac Taylor says that it went from Norwich to Dorchester and Exeter. Mr. H. M. Scarth conjectures that the road crossing the main street of Silchester, which runs east and west, may have been an extension of the Icknield Way from Wallingford to Winchester. In *Social England* Col. Cooper King, following Stukeley, takes the road to Exeter, Totnes, and Land's End; following Bennet, he takes it along the Ridgeway. Elton calls it briefly a road from Norwich through Dunstable and

Silchester to Southampton, and to Sarum and the western districts.

The theorists and conjecturers have done little to ascertain the course of a road which can safely be called the Icknield Way. By far the greater part of the work has been done by men who used chiefly local tradition. Plot in Oxfordshire, Wise in Berkshire, perhaps Robert Morden or an unknown assistant in Hertfordshire. The best of the conjecturers have only linked up the authenticated parts in a probable manner. Most have been too busy with their own views to be anything but benevolent to others. But in 1901 appeared one with no theory and without benevolence, Professor F. Haverfield. In a chapter on "Romano-British Norfolk," in the *Victoria County History* of that county, he pronounces that the Icknield Way is not a Roman road; that it has nothing to do with the Iceni or Norfolk or Suffolk; that the name Icknield and the names like Ickleton and Kenninghall of places on the road, or supposed parts of it, cannot, for philological reasons, be connected with the Iceni. At present he is unanswerable, though his mind is of a type which commands more interest when it affirms than when it denies.

Since the time of Wise little has been done except to add proofs of the antiquity of the road under the Chilterns and the Berkshire Downs. In his day it was known from Royston to Bishopston. Taylor showed that it touched Newmarket, but no more. Mr. Tingey shows that it went through Stoke Holy Cross in Norfolk, but little or nothing has been done to fill the gap between his fragment of Hickling Lane and Newmarket. Even the road between Newmarket and Royston depends for its title only on its respectability as a county and parish boundary. Reaching the Thames there is no certainty of the principal

Icknield Way, near Ipsden, Oxfordshire.

ford; but Streatley must have been one, and from there to Bishopston the main line of the road is clear enough. A man may follow the whole of this road in a few days, and be upon a beaten track if not a hard road everywhere, except for a few hundred yards near Ipsden, and two or three miles from the east side of Lockinge Park. The two lengths north and south of the Thames make a road of uniform character, keeping almost entirely to the chalk, but below the steepest wall of the hills. From Dunstable westward this wall on the left or south of the road is an unmistakable guide to the traveller ; as far as Swyncombe he has only to cling to the foot of the wall and he is on the Icknield Way. Beyond the Thames the Downs make a guiding wall equally clear and continuous. It belongs to what Mr. Harold Peake, in his "Prehistoric Roads of Leicestershire" (*Memorials of Old Leicestershire*), calls the "hill-side" type of road, which "winds along the sides of hills just above the alluvium. Marshes and low-lying ground are avoided, but small streams do not offer so great an obstacle as in the case of the ridge-roads." He compares it with the Pilgrims' Way from Winchester to Canterbury, which it closely resembles, except that it keeps always on the northern slopes, instead of the southern, and commands throughout its course views of a wide, fertile valley northward.

Until the enclosures and the metalling of roads the ruts and hoof-marks of the Icknield Way were probably spread over a width of from a hundred yards to a mile, according to convenience or necessity ; from cntury to century its course might vary even more. Thus the modern road between Kentford and Newmarket is at several points some distance from the Cambridge and Suffolk boundary, which is supposed to follow the Icknield Way.

A deed already mentioned proves that the road was known in Newmarket itself.

Beyond Newmarket the modern road is marked as the Icknield Way, but is only a parish boundary, or rather close to one, for one mile in the first eight, and is not authenticated by any known documents. Nor is any parallel road in the same direction a boundary line. That it is on an old line of road is certain from the number of tumuli which formerly dotted the surrounding heath. It goes through three dykes, two, eight, and thirteen miles from Newmarket, and it has been conjectured both that the dykes defend the road and that the road was made by an invader to pierce the dykes; one antiquary asserts that the fosse of the Brent Ditch "has evidently been filled up to admit the road." From a little beyond the eighth milestone and Fleam Dyke the road is a parish boundary, with very short interruptions between the eleventh and twelfth, as far as the fourteenth, where it becomes the Cambridge and Essex boundary. Turning west beyond the fifteenth, it is followed for some distance by the county boundary, and is thrice rejoined by it, the third time for two miles before entering Royston. By this sharp turning to the west it avoids a Roman camp at Great Chesterford, and passes what Camden called the "ancient little city" of Ickleton, where in his time traces of the "Burrough banks" could plainly be seen. Near Abbey Farm at Ickleton are the remains of a priory. Where it is again a county boundary beyond Ickleton, near "a tumulus opened by the late Lord Braybrooke," it is a farm road, and continues as such in a clear line through arable land and alongside hedges, until it joins the main road into Royston. Here it goes over Burloes Hill, where many indications of ancient burials have been found.

From Royston onwards, as has been seen, the road is marked in a map of 1695. It is mentioned, says Beldam (*Archæological Journal*, XXV), in documents of the twelfth and thirteenth centuries among the monuments of Royston Priory, as "Hickneld" and "Ykenilde." There are hut-circles on the heath to the west, associated with neolithic implements. At Royston, as at Baldock and Tring, gold coins of Cunobelin have been found; and here the road crosses Ermine Street. West of Royston the road is again a county boundary, and goes for miles between many tumuli. "A small Roman habitation" was opened at Slip End near Odsey by Lord Braybrooke. At "Slip Inn" it bounds parishes instead of counties. There is a manor-house and moat at Bygrave, and a tumulus on Metley Hill opposite. Here it passes between two unenclosed parishes, Bygrave and Clothall. It goes along the edge of Baldock, where they have found neolithic and Bronze Age implements and coins of Cunobelin and of "Icenian type," and Roman urns: here is the crossing of Stane Street from Godmanchester to Colchester. For five miles beyond Baldock the road is a parish boundary. It touches a camp at Wilbury Hill, and near it they have found "a great variety of coins of the Roman emperors" and a small copper blade, coins of Constantine, bones and ashes. Ickleford, where it ceases to be a boundary, has produced palæolithic evidences, and the neighbourhood of Hitchin, a mile south, palæolithic and neolithic and late Celtic. Two miles farther on it is a parish boundary for a mile and a half, and then the Hertford and Bedford boundary to the top of Telegraph Hill. Ravenspurgh Castle is a mile north of it on the Barton Hills. It turns along Dray's Ditches and enters the road from Barton to Luton. Here the parish boundary goes straight across, following a lane, to Great Bramingham Farm and, with a break, to Chalton, from which the road might have gone through to Houghton Regis and "the British town of Maiden Bower," and to the north of Dunstable. But the line of the road is continued from Dray's Ditches across the Luton road to Limbury, and over the Lea at Leagrave Marsh, passing, near the moats and the remains of a nunnery at Limbury, the fortification of Waulud's Bank, and the scene of many finds of coins and neolithic implements. This line is clear on Morden's seventeenth-century map. A new street called "Icknield Way" and a footpath lead with recent interruptions into the Luton and Dunstable road, which is for some time a parish boundary. Here it begins to follow under the Downs, which have traces of Celtic huts.

The crossing of Watling Street at Dunstable is vouched for by Dugdale's ancient parchment relating to the foundation of the priory, and by the map of the four royal roads. Between two barrows at Dunstable an ancient trackway used to be traceable to the British camp of Maiden Bower. In the *Catalogue of Ancient Deeds* (I,

Icknield Way, crossing Watling Street, Dunstable.

II, III) there are various references to tenements in the west field or west street extending upon Ikenild - strete, viz. between the time of Edward III and Henry VI. West of Dunstable the direction but not the course of the road is proven by a " letter testimonial " of 1476, where a cross is mentioned standing " in the field of Toternho, the which cross standeth in Ikeneld Stret, to the which cross the way leading from Spilmannstroste directly stretcheth and extendeth, at which place there hath been a cross standing from time that no mind is." Toternhoe parish now includes three-quarters of a mile of the supposed Icknield Way, from the inn at the turning to Kensworth Common, as far as Well Head, and between these points the cross may have stood. Round about the road here are many tumuli on the open downs, and traces of Celtic huts. Toternhoe has a camp not a mile from Maiden Bower, which is in Houghton Regis. A chalk pit three-quarters of a mile north-east of the " Plough " yielded Roman coins in 1769. The " Ykenyldewey " is mentioned in the description of a piece of land at Edlesborough, south-west of Dunstable, in 1348 (Close Rolls, Edward III) ; and the " Ikenyldstret " at Eaton Bray, close by, in the time of Edward II and Richard II (*Catalogue of Ancient Deeds*, I, II, III). The villages of Edlesborough and Eaton Bray are visible a little north of the road. Passing under Beacon Hill and its tumulus, the road enters one from Leighton Buzzard to Aldbury and Wigginton, and out of this road, at points a little north and a little south of the entrance, run two roads marked as the "Lower" and "Upper" Icknield Way, keeping more or less parallel courses as far as Lewknor, where the lower is supposed to join the upper. Neither is a parish or county boundary. At Aston Clinton the "Lower" is crossed and deflected by Akeman Street, which it enters for a mile in a north-westerly direction. Aston has yielded late Celtic pottery. At Weston Turville the "Lower" passes, near the manor-house, a place where a Roman amphora was found in 1855. Akeman Street and several other roads cross and deflect the "Upper" Way. After traversing Wendover you have a camp and barrow on Balcombe Hill, a little to the south. A Danish entrenchment comes down to it from Swyncombe Downs near Britwell. It crosses Grim's Ditch at Foxberry Wood. Flint implements have been found along its course, e.g. in Pulpit Wood at Great Kimble, and at Bledlow. At Whiteleaf, above Monks Risborough, and also above Bledlow, men have carved the turf into crosses, which may be modifications of much earlier phallic forms. British coins, inscribed and uninscribed, have been found at Wendover and Ellesborough, Roman coins between Ipsden and Glebe Farm. Only beyond, where the upper and lower roads are supposed to have united, does the track coincide with a parish boundary, and that but seldom and only for short distances. In Buckinghamshire it was known in the year 903, and mentioned in a "record by King Eadweard, at the request of Duke Aethelfrid, who had lost the original deed by fire, of a grant by Athulf to his daughter Aethelgyth of land at East Hrisan Byrg, or Princes Risborough" (*Cartularium Saxonicum,* No. 603). It is there called "the Icenhylte," and the boundary of the land in question runs along it as far as "the heathen burials." Through Oxfordshire, from Chinnor to Goring and the Streatley ford, the road is authenticated by Plot's map; but routes to the other fords are at present conjectural. Streatley meant the longest way round for travellers going west through Berkshire, but it offered the driest approaches on both hands and the narrowest possible strip of wet land at the crossing. In summer at least Wallingford would attract westward travellers; and there is a thirteenth-century reference in the *Abingdon Chronicle* to Ikeneldstrete as running from Wallingford to Ashbury. Men using this ford would have turned out of the Streatley track at Gypsies' Corner; and here, or a mile or two beyond, near Ipsden, they could branch to Moulsford and the Stokes.

Beyond Streatley there is at first only one road westward on the dry and rising land. This is the main road between Reading and Wantage, with a fork to Wallingford. Mr. Church, of Wantage (1806), pronounced this road to be the Ickleton Way as far as Upton, and his word may be taken to prove at least that this was the local name. For anyone crossing at Streatley and going west under the hills, instead of along the ridge, there is no other road; and even from Moulsford and Wallingford men would be forced, by the river on one side and bad ground on the other, to enter this road at Upton, if not at Blewbury, or before. The ford at Streatley is said to be Roman. Roman pottery has been found in the river, and coins on the south bank. Roman coins by the hundred, dating from 43 B.C. to A.D. 383, have been ploughed up in the neighbourhood. "Near Aston" coins, A.D. 267–74, have been found. They have dug up Roman things in Blewbury Fields, on Hagbourne hill, at Hendred, on Charlton Downs, at Wantage, at Letcombe Regis, in the Dragon Hill near the White Horse, at Woolston, and at Ashbury. Implements of the Bronze Age have been recorded at Cholsey, Moulsford, Blewbury, Hagbourne Hill, Wantage, Letcombe Bassett. Wallingford has yielded palæolithic, neolithic, Bronze Age, and later evidences.

These things, and more that could be mentioned, suggest ancient settlements and communications below the downs. Ickleton Street would seem likely to have been the main line of travel here, and a series of Saxon charters prove that such it was.

A grant of land by Edmund to Ælfric, and by him to Abingdon, shows that an Ichenilde Wege went through Blewbury in 944, and that the Ridgeway was distinct and at some distance from it; a grant in 903 by Eadweard to Tata the son of Æthelhun and by him to Abingdon, one by Edgar to Ælfric and by him to Winchester in 973, and one by Edgar to Ælfstan and by him to Winchester in 970, show it at Harwell (Kemble, *Codex*

Diplomaticus, Nos. 1080, 578, 1273). In the grant of 903 the boundary starts at a brook, the Swyn Brook, and goes along the Harwell Way to the Icenhilde Wey, then up the old wood-way by the east of Harwell Camp to a warren, and so up to the stone on the Ridgeway, then on and back to the Ridgeway, and down on the other side of Harwell Camp to the Icenhilde Wey, farther down to a spring and an elder bed, evidently in the low land. This shows that the Icknield Way was a road running between the Ridgeway and the lowest land. A grant of land made in 955 by Eadred to Ælfheh and by him to Abingdon at Compton Beauchamp (Kemble, No. 1172) proves the same. The boundary starts at the Ridgeway, and goes to the Icenhilde Wey, and on to the Swyn Brook, and back again past a barrow to the Icenhilde Wey, and up to the Ridgeway, and over hills, slades, and a green way back to Wayland's Smithy. A grant of Æthelstan to Abingdon, of land in Woolston, Compton, and Ashbury (Kemble, No. 1129), and another (No. 1168) mention as landmarks Ikenilde Strete, then what is probably Uffington Castle, and other places on the downs; then what is probably Ælfred's Castle and two barrows and the Ikenilde Strete again, and finally a rush bed in the low land. A grant by Æthelwulf to Winchester and Bishop Stigand in 854 of lands at Wanborough (Kemble, No. 1053) describes a boundary passing downs and coombes to the source of the Hlyd (there is a Lyde spring at Ashbury), along the stream to a ditch, past the Dorc stream, the Smit stream, and a black pit, over the Icknield Way at or near some heathen burial place, and so to down country with a white pit, two stones, and a coombe, etc.—and from a study of the district Mr. Harold Peake concludes that "the Icknield Way crossed the parish very near the modern road which on the Ordnance Map bears this name, though I fancy it ran originally a few hundred yards to the north." It is clear, then, that the Icknield Way ran as far as Wanborough between the highest and lowest ground along a course similar to that of Wise's Ickleton Street. The road mentioned must either be Wise's road or another of similar course which has been superseded by it in name and use, and can hardly be other than that now called on the Ordnance Map the Port Way.

Thus the road from Newmarket—or at least from Royston—by Streatley to Wanborough parish is a venerable and continuous one, which bore almost the same name at its extremities—Ykenildeweie at Newmarket in the time of Henry III, Icenhilde Weg at Wanborough in 854. That it is Icknield Street, one of the "four royal roads," is proved only by its coming out of the east and going westward, and by its crossing Watling Street at Dunstable, as does the Ykenildstrete of the thirteenth-century map. Unlike the other three roads, the Icknield Way appears not to have been Romanized at any point, and, assuming that it had in the Middle Ages the importance suggested by its rank with these roads, its primitive character would explain its decay. Nothing rescued it as pilgrimages rescued that part of an ancient east-and-west road now known as the Pilgrims' Way from Winchester to Canterbury (*The Old Road*, by Hilaire Belloc). Its western object had apparently been so deeply lost in Drayton's time that the poet took it to Southampton, though whether this line is to be traced to Geoffrey of Monmouth's bold definition or to contemporary usage cannot easily be decided. That this road through Newmarket and Streatley is the one in Drayton's mind is certain.

Of the other roads called Icknield Street, most, if not all, of them difficult, where not impossible, to connect with this road as continuations or as branches, one is particularly interesting here.

Dr. Macray's "MS. Catalogue of Magdalen College Deeds" contains several mentions of Ikenildwey or Hykenyldewey in descriptions of boundaries at Enham, near Andover, in Hampshire. One belonging to 1270 refers to land "in the east field of Enham, on the north of the highway called Ikenildwey"; another of 1317 to two acres of land in Enham Regis in a field called Bakeleresbury; "of the which one acre lies between the land of Gilbert Slyk on either side, extending south to Ikenildwe . . ."; one of 1337 to arable land in the fields of Andover, of which half an acre extends "above Hykenyldewey to the east," between other estates in the north and south, while another acre in the same field extends "above Laddrewey to the north." I conclude from these descriptions that the Hykenyldewey here ran east and west, and it is not a region of winding roads. Batchelor's Barn and Walworth cottages, about a mile east of Andover, seem to contain memories of " La Werthe," " La Walwert," and " Bakeleresbury." Both the barn and the cottages lie close to the south side of the Harrow Way, which here goes east and west on its way from Farnham to Weyhill. Walworth cottages are on the east of the intersection of the Harrow Way and the north-westward Roman road from Winchester to Wanborough Nythe, and not a mile south of the intersection of this Roman road with the north-eastward Port Way from Old Sarum to Silchester. Between the Harrow Way and the Port Way, and in this part of its course almost parallel with them, is a road from Stoke and Newbury. One of these roads is perhaps the road referred to in the deeds as "Hykeynldewey." The Harrow Way, which still bears its name in the neighbourhood, is not likely to have been the road. The Port Way appears to be purely Roman. If the road from Stoke were the Icknield Way, it might have connected Streatley with Winchester and Southampton, yet if it went to Winchester and Southampton, it can hardly have been the road which is several times called Ikenilde Street in records of the perambulations of the Hampshire forests. The survey of Buckholt Forest, under Edward I, for example, contains the passage: " Begin at the Deneway . . . and so always by the divisions of the counties of Southampton and Wilts to th' Ikenilde Street, and thence by the same to La Pulle"; and "from Pyrpe-mere to th' Ikenilde and so by the same road to Holeweye." This road I cannot identify, but a road touching both Enham and Buckholt Forest would probably reach Old Sarum.

There is an Icknield Street, marked as such on the Ordnance Map, going north from Weston subedge to Bidford, and, after a gap, from Stadley north towards Birmingham. It goes for some miles parallel to a much higher Ridgeway. It leaves the Fosse Way four miles south of Stow-in-the-Wold, near Bourton-on-the-Water, and is the road described by Codrington as Ricknild Street. But Codrington refers to a part of it—where the railway crosses it at Honeybourne station—as called Ricknild or Icknield Street, and to the lane north of Bidford going towards Alcester as Icknield Street. This road, or a longer one in part coinciding with it, was first called Icknield Street by Ralph Higden in the fourteenth century. It was one of his four royal roads, and went from St. David's to Worcester, Birmingham, and Derby. Some of the manuscripts of his work called the road Ryckneld, which spelling may or may not have been due to the local knowledge of a scribe; both English translators or their scribes retain the R, calling the road Rykenildes strete or Rikenilde Street. Mr. W. H. Duignan (*Notes on Staffordshire Place Names*) quotes references to this road in the twelfth century—between Lichfield and Derby—as Ikenhilde, Ykenild, and Ricnelde; in the thirteenth century as Rikelinge and Ykenilde; in the fourteenth century as Rykeneld strete. He also gives instances which seem to prove that there were unconnected roads known as Ricknield Street in the thirteenth century; and mentions a place now called Thorpe Salvin, lying on no known Ricknield Street, but once known as Rikenild-thorp. Selden found a deed mentioning Ricknield Street as a boundary near Birmingham, and Dugdale one of 1223 relating to Hilton Abbey.

The *Eulogium* of 1362, when it does not call Higden's road Belinstrete, calls it Hykeneldstret, though when Gale quotes it he makes it Rykeneld-strete. Stukeley calls it "the Ricning Way," and complains of Plot for calling it Icknil Way; yet he himself heard it called the Hickling Street near the crossing of Watling Street. Holinshed calls it "Ikenild or Rikenild." In the time of the second and third Edwards there were men named after Ikenilde or Hikenilde strete (Pat. Rolls) in Worcestershire. One of them was a man of Alvechurch, which lies west of the road between Stadley and Birmingham; and there was an Ikeneld street in the sixteenth century within the lordship of Allechurche in Worcestershire.

Drayton first distinguished between an eastern Icknield Street and a western Ricknield Street. He evidently knew the Icknield Way along the Chilterns, and his words about Rikneld Street as coming from Cambria's farther shore until the road

> "On his midway did me in England meet,"

suggest that he knew the road as a Warwickshire man, and that his distinction was not wantonness or the precision of ignorance. Gale accuses the road of taking the name of Ickle or Icknild Street without any just title. Guest also believes that the western road "gradually attached to itself the name of Icknield Street" as a famous name to which it had no right. Wise, in search of something to help him, suggests Hickling as the origin of the name, but knowing of Ryknield, he is tempted also by Rickley in Essex—confesses the temptation —and "must now beg leave to call" the road "the Great Ickle or Rickle way." This use of Rickling reminds me of a woman living in a cottage beside the Ridgeway, near Chiseldon. I asked her the name of the road, and she said, with some hesitation, "The Rudgeway." I asked why it was so called, and she said she did not know. I asked where it went, and she answered, "Oh, over there!"—pointing west,"—to Rudge, I suppose," Rudge being near Westbury. An antiquary in the *Gentleman's Magazine* (1787) comfortably explains the variation as due to the British particle "yr" prefixed. But no one has found a Ricknield or a Rickling or any such name along the course of the road from Newmarket to Wanborough.

It seems likely that Icknield, like Watling and Ermine, was a generic name for a road, whether due to its use by cattle, to Professor Bradley's Lady Icenhild, or to something else. One such road in Worcestershire and the west, and another in the east tending westward, were possibly at one time well known as continuous routes over long stretches of country. The two could be connected. Ermine Street passed through Wanborough Nythe at the west end of the Icknield Way from East Anglia, went north-west to Cirencester, and thence both north-east to Stow-on-the-Wold where it touched the Ricknield Street and the Fosse Way, and north-west to Gloucester, and so to Worcester or to Kentchester and the south-west of Wales. Another ancient road from near Tring, the Akeman Street, would take travellers on the Icknield Way due west to Cirencester, where they could branch as they pleased to Gloucester and Wales or the north. Thus at both ends of Ermine Street and Akeman Street or their continuations there were roads known as Icknield Street ; it is even possible that the whole system was officially given the one name of Icknield Street, and such a system might fitly be called a royal road. An eastern extension of the road to a depôt and several ports in Norfolk is practically certain, though it has not yet been discovered or satisfactorily reconstructed. A south-western or western extension beyond Wanborough is almost equally certain. There is no need to look for a road that is all of one type. Without antiquarianism or modern regularity only common and continued travel throughout its course can preserve a road. Even during this extended use of it variants will be discovered from time to time and used as alternatives or substitutes. As soon as this use ceases portions of the road begin to decay, and soon those few having the old need for it will have found another way. Each kind of civilization doubtless has its own special kind of road, and gradually old roads are so transformed or combined as to form such a road. But invaders or newly organized people have to take what roads they find, unless they have Roman will, forethought, and resource to make their own; though by good fortune men suddenly needing a road may find an old one ready as did the pilgrims from the south and west to Canterbury who used the Pilgrims' Way. Men wishing to travel from east to west, especially in the south of England, would have found many tracks and roads of all types ready to be linked so as to form a connection between important points of trade, government, or religion. When it became possible to traverse England safely, meeting foreign faces and strange tongues but subjects of one king, traders and travellers would piece together according to need the old roads which different ages had confirmed—the high and most ancient roads like the Ridgeway and the Harrow Way, late roads skirting the bases of the hills, pure Roman roads fearing nothing, and Romanized trackways. The Icknield Way may have been such a combination. The Danes might have combined it with the Ridgeway in 1005, when they burnt Wallingford and went by Cholsey and Cuckhamsley to Kennet. They probably used the road along the Chilterns when they burnt Thetford and Cambridge and turned south to the Thames; and other parts of it when they stole inland from their ships through Norwich to Thetford. Sweyn may have gone along it when he went to Wallingford, and so over the Thames westward to Bath, where the western men submitted and gave hostages and he became king of the whole people. Giraldus may have trodden it in South Wales. At an earlier age, as Mr. Moray

Whiteleaf Cross.

Williams has suggested, the Icknield Way might have been the line of the Iceni in their alleged migration westward, after the defeat of Boadicea. It should have been Imogen's pathway to Milford Haven. There are not many early references to the travel upon the road. It would be used chiefly by traders and travellers from a distance. Plot remarked that it passed through no towns or villages in Oxfordshire, and this, in his day, made it convenient for stealers of cattle. A road used by strange travellers and robbers waiting for them was not a likely one for small settlements and local use. When it was spoken of as the way the oxen go—unless the phrase implied a road along which came oxen from a distance—it may already have been degenerating. Guest says: "Your guide will talk of the long lines of pack-horses that once frequented the 'Ickley Way,' as if they were things of yesterday; and a farmer in the Vale of Aylesbury told me . . . that in the popish times they used to go on pilgrimage along it from Oxford to Cambridge." Messrs. Jordan and Morris (*Introduction to the Study of Local History and Antiquities*) speak of the road as connecting the flint-knappers' settlement at Brandon with Avebury and Stonehenge: "The men of Wiltshire would wish to obtain flint instruments from Brandon; men from Brandon to have access to Avebury and Stonehenge." But Wiltshire men would not go to Suffolk in search of flints except for a wager.

The Icknield Way is sufficiently explained as the chief surviving road connecting East Anglia and the whole eastern half of the regions north of the Thames, with the west and the western half of the south of England. For the men of Norfolk, Suffolk, Cambridge, Bedford, Hertford, Buckingham, and Oxford, it did what the Harrow Way did for men of Kent, Surrey, Sussex, and East Hampshire.

CHAPTER III

FIRST DAY—THETFORD TO NEWMARKET, BY LACKFORD AND KENTFORD

As nearly everybody was agreed that the Icknield Way, coming from the Norfolk ports, probably crossed the River Thet and the Little Ouse at Thetford in that county, I went to Thetford. In the railway train I asked a man who knew all the country about him whether he knew the Icknield Way, but he did not. He knew where the oaks and pines grew best and what they fetched, the value of the land, the crops on an acre of it and what they fetched. He knew men's rents and what each farm cost when it changed hands last. He knew also the men living and dead, and the lives they lived, what they were worth, and whose bed they died in. He was a man himself, a vast handsome fellow nearing sixty, well bearded, whiskered, and moustached, but not so as to hide full red lips and small, cheerful, and penetrating dark eyes. He weighed eighteen stone and a half and was not scant of breath, though he smoked strong tobacco rapidly in a large pipe. After much about the price of potatoes, etc., that came in at one ear and bolted straight out of the other, he told about himself and his family. Everyone at the railway stations knew him, and I suppose he thought I should naturally not wish to remain ill-informed. He was the youngest but one of six brothers, all weighing over sixteen stone; and his two sisters weighed over fourteen. He himself had eight children, the sons above six feet in height, the daughters above five-feet-eight—all of them persons who would not be blown away in a storm. His father before him was six-feet-three and weighed seventeen stone. After a time, pointing to a satchel with my name and address on it, he said:—

"Do you know anyone of the name of Fencer in your neighbourhood?"

"No," I said.

"Her father," he said, "used to own the Largease Mill. Polly Fencer. Very likely he has gone away now. She may be dead. It is twenty-five years ago that I am thinking of, and I will tell you what made me ask. My next brother was in love with her twenty-five years ago. She was a well-educated person, good-looking, and had the nicest temper of anyone I ever met, but not soft or at all weak. She liked my brother; but she was a companion to some lady and she did not want to marry at once. He did, however, and when she refused to be in a hurry he got cool for a time. In that cool fit he married another woman and had plenty of time to repent it. He lived with her twenty years and more, and she was always ailing. He never cared much about her and now she is dead, and it struck me, seeing the address on your bag, that perhaps if Polly was alive and free and hadn't altered her mind, my brother might be glad to marry her. Certainly he couldn't do a better thing than marry Polly. I know he never forgot her. But twenty-five years is a long time, and she may be married herself. . . . I should have liked to see him marry Polly, one of the nicest women that ever I saw. . . .

"I used to be very fond of walking myself," he

Castle Hill, Thetford.

said, changing the subject. "And I still do a lot of it. It is very good for the health. I suppose you are walking for your health."

As he perceived that I was not in business he assumed that I was taking a dose of walking, one of the most expensive medicines, and, as he believed, one of the best. I left him behind me in Thetford.

This was a most pleasant ancient town, built of

flints, full of turns and corners and yards. It smelt of lime trees and of brewing. At the east edge was a green "Castle Hill" and a surrounding rampart without a castle, and between the ramparts, round about the hill, a level green where people rest or play in sunshine or under elm, ash, and sycamore. Beside the steep artificial mound, so huge and uncouth, men mowing the grass looked smaller than ever, the children playing more beautiful, and both more transitory. The dark hill seemed a monster watching them at their play and work, as if some day it would swallow them up. It was like a personification of stupid enormous time. Yet this ponderous symbol did not spoil the pleasantness of the grass and trees and the green hill and the little town, but rather increased it; and I walked backwards and forwards lest I should forget that I had been to Thetford, a place sometimes burnt, sometimes fortified, by the Danes, and once a bishop's see. These things made the old brewery seem older, the lime trees sweeter, the high-walled lanes darker, as I walked about. One of the lanes, Castle Lane, which goes through the ramparts of the castle, is possibly part of the Icknield Way. As you stand at the east edge of the town, a little past the Castle hill, a lane comes slanting from the north-east over the railway to an open, dusty place, at a meeting of five ways, a "five went way." This lane, now only a mile long to where it is cut short by the Kilverstone and Brettenham road and having no obvious continuation to the north-east, is the Green Lane, or Clover Lane, which has been suggested as a Norfolk portion of the Icknield Way. At the south end of it, in 1870, were found remains of Celtic and Roman pottery. Castle Lane takes up the line of Green Lane and leads through the east edge of the town towards the rivers. Before leaving the town by it, I noticed on the right hand a very strange fish on a sign-board, a very curly fish, with curly whiskers, three curled plumes on his back, and a curled tail; and he was himself curled and boldly painted withal; but whether this fish or the landlord was named Mullett I have forgotten. My apparent road took me southward over the Thet, and then the Ouse, by two low bridges called the Nuns' Bridges. Chestnuts darkened the clear water of Thet. Between the two rivers was only a narrow space of grass and buttercups. Here, and a little east towards Place Farm, is the gravel which fitted this spot for a ford. Beyond the Ouse the main road goes straight away southward to the Workhouse, the open, sandy heath, and ultimately Bury St. Edmunds. On the left was the isolated doorway of a vanished nunnery, and Place Farm standing within a wide, low-walled space. I turned to the right along a road parallel with the river and divided from it by a narrow hedgeless band of grass. This is supposed by Mr. W. G. Clarke to be the Icknield Way, and he has sketched it over the Bury and Thetford road north of the gasworks, near where the remains of a British settlement were found in 1870. But I found nothing to save me from going on to the main road to Mildenhall and Newmarket and then following that for two miles. On the ten miles between Thetford and Mildenhall there is nothing but Elveden Church, motor-cars, milestones, and dust; and Mildenhall is only the half-way village to Newmarket. It is a straight road easily provoked to a fierce whiteness, and it goes through a dry heathy land planted with limes and parallelograms of fir trees. Nevertheless, a nightingale was singing at noon in the blaze of a strong sun close to the left side of the road, not a mile out of Thetford. His voice in the heat was like the milky kernel of a hard, bearded nut.

Less than half a mile past the second milestone, and just over the Suffolk border, I took the opportunity of leaving that road by entering a private drive apparently to Elveden Hall. This was at least in the right direction for Lackford, the next ford, near which the Icknield Way is satisfactorily ascertained. In three-quarters of a mile the drive emerged into a road coming from the main road I had left, and going east to Barnham. I turned to the left along this to reach Marmansgrave Wood, which sounded old, and at that point, as I hoped, a cart track, crossing the road from north to south, looked possible. As it fell out, this track was a parish boundary and the boundary between the hundreds of Blackbourn and Lackford; and for more than half its course it was on one side or the other of an oak or fir plantation. I went southward along it, down the east edge of the long fir plantation marked on the map as "New Barnham Slip." It was a broad and hedgeless track, often riddled by rabbit burrows which were masked by nettles. At its best it was a rough, tussocky sheaf of cartways. Everywhere sand and flints, parallelograms of fir trees, nettles, and more nettles and the smell of nettles. Rarely it passed a square, now, or several years ago, given to corn. I like nettles, especially with elder trees in blossom above them, as at Lackford Road Heath, half-way along. There was also some gorse. The road was not straight, but wound along in a series of straight lines, slightly up and down, but usually on the high level sand with views of nothing else. I had no company but pewit and stone-curlew and wheatear for those seven miles, and neither passed a house nor saw one anywhere. The sun blazed from the sky overhead and the sand underfoot; it burnt the scent out of the pines as in an oven; it made the land still and silent; but it wrenched no word or thought of blasphemy out of me. On the other hand, I felt no benevolence towards the planters of trees in straight lines; for by doing this they had destroyed the possible sublimity of this sandy land, and at the same time increased its desolation by the contrasting verdure of foliage and the obviously utilitarian arrangement. It was country which, if I owned it, I should gladly exchange with the War Office for Salisbury Plain. For if the nettles, the rabbit holes, and the elders were exceptionally good they could be equalled. The rabbits seemed to love the track as in other places they love tumuli, and for a distance they had wiped out its resemblance to a road.

Crossing the Brandon and Wordwell road at

Shelterhouse Corner or Elveden Gap, I reached the east end of the Icklingham belt of firs. From near the west end of this belt goes a south-westerly path called "Pilgrim's Path," down to Icklingham All Saints' Church. This is said not to be the Icknield Way, though Icklingham, partly on account of its name, and partly on account of its great age and Roman villa, has been alleged to be on the road. Two miles east of my road at Lackford Road Heath is a "Traveller's Hill," marked by a tumulus, but this is an east-and-west road and ends at a farm. I continued over Jennet's Hill and along the edge of a second and greater Icklingham belt, and past some cultivated fields, on the right, sunk two yards or so below the level of the track. Then I dipped down among corn and deeper grass, and between good hedges at last, towards the River Lark, the cool valley, and the broader woods of Lackford and Cavenham. At the foot of the descent a road crosses to West Stow, and in half a mile passes a gravel pit and the place where Anglo-Saxon coins, weapons, and arms have been found. After this crossing there were water meadows, with swift crystal flashing among buttercups and flag blossom, the home of snipe. The great meadow on the right is called Rampart Meadow, because of the sudden lift of the land at its far side, which seems to be ringed like an old camp with ramparts. Just before the river the road became merged in the main road from Mildenhall to Bury St. Edmunds. Alongside the bridge was the ford, and the path to it was hollowed out beside the road on the south. Over the bridge the boundary leaves the road and joins the Lark.

Lackford is a village that straggles along a mile of road with such intervals of foliage that I thought I was past the end of it when I came to where I

Bridge and Ford, Lackford.

could get tea. There was no inn; but the shop was better than the inn could have been. My hostess was one of those most active, little, stoutish and cheerful women who never go out if they can help it. Being descended from suffering and sometimes roofless generations, they seem to see no reason for returning to inclement nature when they have a good digestion and a water-tight roof; they make good jam and good tea. There were a number of things I should haveseen near Lackford, such as the burial mound, north of Culford Church, wittily called the "Hill of Health," and the road between Pakenham and Stowlangtoft called Bull Road, and some of the moats, at Maulkin's Hall and other "Halls" of Suffolk. But the Icknield Way turned sharp to the right out of the road I had taken, opposite Lower Farm, soon after the ford of the Lark. When it was more important than the eastward road to Bury the Way curved round westward beyond the river, and its old course is marked by a depression through the furze on the right, which finally reaches the present road and is lost in it.

My road was now an ordinary white road between hedges, but with a furzy heath on both sides beyond the hedges. It had no grassy borders, but at the turning to Lackford manor-house there was a little triangular common on the left, of grass, gorse, hawthorns, and an ash tree. On the right there was a larger common, called Clamp's Heath. On my left I saw corn and a field of pale sainfoin extending to the edge of a dark oak wood. The road was, if anything, slightly embanked over this level ground. After passing the Heath it had grassy borders and low hedges and corn on both sides, and then, after a short distance, no border, and on the right no hedge. Where it descended towards the woods of Cavenham it was sunk a little and had a left-hand border of grass. Just before this I saw the first chalk pit under the road on my left, with wild rose and elder on its floor. At Cavenham a new flat bridge of two arches crossed a tiny tributary of the Lark ; but on the left of this was an old single arch about seven feet broad of narrow bricks, still

Near Cavenham.

firm but all grass-grown over its high curved crown which passengers used to mount like a barrel. The new bridge probably took the ford's place. At Cavenham the road went under the trees of Cavenham Park—oak, beech, elm and sycamore, ash and aspen. Turtle-doves were cooing unseen. The house was some way off, the church farther, the village yet farther along a by-road. At each turning there was an open space for trees and men, for example, at the two ways down to Lark Hall. Beyond the second of these the road was lined by beech trees and wych elms standing in grass: it was cool, but gave a view of sunlit barley between the trunks, and soon afterwards of an undulating lowland, heath and corn, and wooded ridges on the right; while on the left the land fell away and I felt the curve of the earth, the wooded horizon being lower than the road. Before reaching Tuddenham Corner the bank of bird's-foot trefoil was wide enough for a path; only on the left was there a hedge, on the right was tall barley. Past Tuddenham Corner the road was narrow and shaded by beech trees of half a century's growth; it had hedges and grassy borders, and down the middle two lines of grass between the ordinary course of the horses' feet and the wheels. On both sides were many long, straight plantations of trees, but in a low, cultivated country where they gave little offence. Presently the road touched a tumulus on the left, and drew near another on the right. Then it was crossed by the Great Eastern Railway, and turning sharper to the right than probably it used to, went due west towards Kentford. Being now a highway between Newmarket and Bury St. Edmunds, it was broader, and had also grassy margins of twice its own width, and beeches in the hedgerows.

Until this I had met and passed nobody, nor had anyone passed me; no man of Lackford or Cavenham, or vagrant bound for Norwich or Newmarket; no long-lost sailor son whom I could tell of his expectant mother selling roses at Piccadilly Circus.

Kentford.

At Kentford motor-cars tyrannically owned the road. Here were men going into the "Fox and Bull," or standing contented by the "Old Cock." In the shade of the old flint church tower and the chestnuts of the churchyard someone was cheerfully clipping grass at evenfall. I looked up and saw a greyhound as a weather vane, and it was running northward. A ford went through the Kennett and a new bridge over it, alongside of great fragments of an old one. Just beyond, at the cool heart of the dusty roadside shrubberies, a nightingale was singing in oblivion.

From Kentford the road ran straight for four miles into Newmarket, taking with it the Suffolk and Cambridge boundary now on its right and now on its left. Telegraph posts and trees accompanied it, and below them very broad, rough margins, half overgrown by thorns and young elms, and marked by half a dozen parallel footpaths. The old course of the road from the third milestone was doubtless the green track on the right, divided from the new by a broken hedge; for it is this that the boundary follows. Before the second milestone this track traversed the new and was continued thenceforward by a beech grove shadowing deep, narrow horse-paths to the first milestone and the beginning of the Newmarket red brick. On the right no hedge came between the road and an open country sloping down to the treeless fenland of Fordham, Wicken, and Soham, where fifty feet above sea-level makes a hill. Nearest the road were plains from which tumuli have long been smoothed to make an exercising ground for horses.

By the first milestone a child came running up to me to ask if I had found a penny among the trees, and I did not until afterwards suspect that this was a brilliant variation from straightforward begging.

Newmarket.

As I came into Newmarket before dark, but after the closing of shops, the long wide street and a strange breed of men standing or slowly walking about on its pavements made me feel that scarcely after a dozen reincarnations should I enter Newmarket and be at home. The man who discovered that we are "all God's creatures" had an uncanny eye for resemblance, and I often doubt the use of the discovery, without disputing its accuracy. Everyone was talking of horses except those who preferred lords and professional golfers. I saw some caddies industriously swallowing temperance hot drinks instead of beer, in the hope of earning as much as James Braid at some distant time. As for the horsy men, they seemed to understand lords as well as horses, so well as to illustrate the saying, "To know all is to pardon all": nay! to go beyond that, to admire all, and to believe that men are more or less worthy as they are more or less lords. One of them was imitating the bad language of Lord ——, and it was admitted perfect; but I can quite believe that to be a lord is very different from being able to imitate one after a glass of ale. There can be little doubt that to the influence of either lords or horses, or perhaps both, we must attribute the brilliant beggar at the first milestone. A Scotch baker directed me to a place—"It is not very elaborate, but it is clean"—where I could get a bed such as I could afford.

I lay awake for some time listening to the motor-cars. Most of them rushed through the town; a few came there to rest and silence; others paused for a minute only with drumming suspense. I thought I should not easily tire of these signals from unknown travellers. Not that I spent much time on definite and persistent conjecture as to who they were, whence they had come, and whither and why they travelled. I was too sleepy, though at any time such a labour would have been irksome. No ; I was more than content to let these noises compose a wordless music of mystery and adventure within my brain. The cars could bring together lovers or enemies or conspirators so swiftly that their midnight alarums suggest nothing else. It is hard to connect their subjugated frenzy with mere stupid haste. The little light steals through a darkness so vast that the difference between a star and a lantern is nothing to it. The thing is so suitable for a great adventure that straightway the mind conceives one. Hark ! on a winter's night the sound and the idea are worthy of the storm and in harmony with it :—

> Hark 'tis an elfin storm from fairyland,
> Of haggard seeming but a boon indeed. . . .

It was easy to imagine myself the partner in magnificent risks quite outside my own experience, and to feel the glory and even the danger with no touch of pain, whilst I lay as careless as the friendly near neighbourhood of sleep could make me. The touch of arrogance in the voice of the motor is to its credit by night. In a measure it revives the romantic and accepted arrogance of horn and trumpet. It gives at least an outward bravery which has long been dropping away from drivers of horses. I do not disparage the sound of hoofs and wheels and the private voice of a solitary traveller on the dark roads, but there is something melancholy in it, and more endurance than enterprise. . . . But, above all, the sounds of the motor-car have added immensely to the London night, at least for good sleepers with minds at ease. Formerly, to those out of the Covent Garden routes, the only sound of night travel at all provoking to the mind was the after-midnight hansom's clatter, which challenged conjecture more often than imagination; I pictured most likely a man with bleared eyes and a white shirt who had let his cigar out—at most, a man whose achievement was behind rather than before him; and certainly I was always very well content to be in bed. But the motor-horn is turbulent and daring, though it may be innocent to say so. Even if it is coming home there is a proud possibility of distance left behind, and either it seems that the arrivers have not returned for nothing or the sudden stop suggests at the least a sublimity of dejection from proud heights. As to the car setting out in darkness, it gathers to itself all the pomp of setting out, as we have imagined or read of it in stories of soldiers, travellers or lovers, and as we have experienced it when children, going to fish or to find bird's nests or mushrooms, and as we still fancy it would be for ourselves, were we ever to advance towards adventures. I suppose, also, that the speed of a motor-car, to the outsider, unconsciously suggests a race, an unknown end, an untold prize. . . . These thoughts and mere listening to the horns and machinery occupied me and led on to sleep in such a manner that I ignored a man next door imitating a gramophone quite seriously, and in less than half an hour I was asleep and began to dream drivel.

CHAPTER IV

SECOND DAY—NEWMARKET TO ODSEY, BY ICKLETON AND ROYSTON

NEXT morning I paid two shillings and set out at six o'clock. So far as is known the Icknield Way, which certainly went through Newmarket, is the central street and London road, and along this I mounted out of the town. The road was a straight and dusty one, accompanied by a great multitude of telegraph wires, on which corn buntings were singing their dreary song. On the right was the main stretch of Newmarket Heath, then a few gentle green slopes, with clusters of ricks and squares of corn, rising to a low wooded ridge far off. It was beginning to be hot, though it was windy and the deep blue of the sky was visible only through folds in the hood of grey clouds.

There were dusty tracks for exercising horses on both sides of the road. I like to see fine horses running at full speed. To see this sight, or hounds running on a good scent, or children dancing, is to me the same as music, and therefore, I suppose, as full of mortality and beauty. I sat down for some time watching the horses.

Beyond the second milestone, and just before the turning to the right for Cambridge, the road passed through the Devil's Ditch, a deep ditch with a

Devil's Ditch.

high bank on the Newmarket edge of it, stretching several miles on either side of the way from north-west to south-east in a straight line. At the gap made by the road stood what seemed to be old turnpike houses. Beyond the ditch the road was a hedged one, shaded by beeches on both sides, and having borders of deep, dusty grass, in which stood the telegraph posts. The long, narrow copse of beech on the right was not strictly closed, but remained unspoilt and tenanted by doves. Yet it was not long before I began to look out for a cart to carry me over the next six miles of the straight road. Such a road is tiring, because either the eye or the mind's eye sees long, taunting, or menacing lengths before it, and is brought into conflict with sheer distance, and the mind is continually trying to carry the body over this distance with her own celerity, and being again and again defeated and more and more conscious of defeat, becomes irritated, if not happily numbed, by the importunate monotony.

This was country, moreover, which the unaided eye could easily explore. It lay open and without mystery. Nothing had to be climbed or quested for. Therefore still more did the legs resent doing what wheels or other legs could do far better. Any wheeled vehicle, from a motor-car to a legless beggar's trolley, would help a man through this country. In Wiltshire or Cardiganshire there is nothing so good as your own legs, even if they are bad. But in Cambridgeshire I recommend elephant, camel, horse, mule, donkey, motor-car, waggon, or cart, anything except a covered cab or a pair of hobnailed shoes.

A fine region spread out upon the right as I was approaching Six Mile Bottom—a sweep of arable, mostly corn-covered, but with reddish, new-ploughed squares, and here and there a team at work, rising up to a copse or two on the low ridges—not a building visible but a windmill—and far beyond these, blue hills. A very simple country it was, that might have been moulded by a strong north wind when the land was docile as snow. Over it hung a sky of perfect summer and a sun like a god that made me ashamed to crawl as habit and the necessity of writing a book compelled me to do. It was a country for clouds, but there was none. Had there been, I should not have been so well acquainted with the hard, straight road, often slightly embanked, or having depressions on either side, and in the right-hand one several well-worn paths. By the turning to Weston Colville and West Wratting it went level and straight as usual. On the left the corn was hedgeless; on the right a low hedge separated me from ploughland and the windmill on a mile-distant ridge; and the depression on the left was thrice the width of the road, and used as a cart track, with merely a white centre and ruts among the flowers of plantain and lady's slipper. Many larks were singing. I became a connoisseur in road-sides, and noticed each change, as that when the road was cut or embanked it usually lost its breadth of margin, and that now there was a hedge on both hands instead of one, and in them roses—the pink roses which have the pure, slender perfume connected by the middle-aged with youth.

Past the eighth milestone the road went through

Fleam Dyke, which is shorter than the Devil's Ditch, because the fen to which it stretches northward is nearer. The ditch is on the far side, a green farm track goes along the mound on the near or Newmarket side. Just before it I saw a green

Fleam Dyke.

way, a parish boundary, branching up out of my road eastward between separate thorns and making over the highland to the valley of the Stour. Beyond the dyke was another fine open cornland northward, lines of trees down its slopes, woods on its ridges, and the tall chimneys of Cambridge six miles away. On the other hand a beech plantation lined the road and shadowed the grassy edge on which I walked. After the beeches there were wayside roses, and a low hedge and still a broad, grassy border, where the short-tailed young blackbirds hurried before me among the paper wrappers of sausages, etc., thrown out by motorists from Cambridge.

On my right was an artificial wall of turf going in the same direction as the road. This might have been an ancient earthwork, if the map had not said "Old Railway." A disused railway embankment gave me more pleasure than a prehistoric dyke. It was also charming in itself, and had thorns prettily growing on its green slopes. Soon it was changed to a cutting, and, above it, a little round rise crowned by eight poor firs in a tragic group, a few hundred yards from the road. Past the tenth milestone the main road reaches Worsted Lodge and crosses the straight line of a Roman road from Grantchester and Godmanchester. The line of my road is continued by a lesser way to Babraham and Pampisford, but the road itself turns abruptly from a south-westerly almost to a southerly course, yet still straight. Nearly all the roads hereabout were as straight as if Roman, the low and even land offering no impediments. There was one, for example, parallel with the Roman road and crossing the Icknield Way exactly at the tenth milestone, having come down from Fulbourn Valley Farm alongside a regiment of beeches, and continuing, after an interruption by a kitchen garden, to Gunner's Hall beyond. Between this and the Roman road, at the wayside, was a long, flint-tiled building of respectable age, with a mansard roof, small latticed windows in three tiers, and a louvre on top like a small oast cone. The line of the old railway continued to be marked by a slight bank and thickets of thorns. My road had broad green borders which the copse of Grange Farm interrupted. There were now more copses, and the land was more broken up, though still mainly supporting corn and hurdled sheep. At Bourn Bridge, near the twelfth milestone, there was a ford through the Granta, shaded by elms and poplars and occupied by cattle swishing their tails in silence. At the milestone the common road to Royston branches off to the right with broad green borders, but my way lay straight on over the new railway by Pampisford station and through Brent Ditch. After the thirteenth milestone the old railway had gathered quite a copse of ash and thorn and brier about it. Near the fourteenth milestone I began to see a pleasant valley land below on the right, and groves marking the Cam's course by the spires of Hinxton and Ickleton, and beyond them gentle, bare hills with crowns of trees. At this milestone I saw myriads of a most delicate blue flax shuddering in the wind. Here Essex comes up to the road and pursues it to Ickleton, even though at Stump Cross it turns sharp to the right out of the London road and becomes a lane to Ickleton, a green lane with white ruts making for the church, and crossing an artificial embankment which turned out to be the old railway again. My road forded the

Cam at Ickleton. This was a quiet white and grey village, built partly about the road which encircles the church, but chiefly on both sides of a road leading west. The walls were of flint or of plaster, sometimes decorated with patterns

Ickleton.

in line, and there was abundant thatch. Here and there the cottages were interrupted and a gateway opened into a farm-yard. The church, a flint one, was as cool as it was old, and full of christened sunlight and the chirping of sparrows. There were many tablets in it to the memory of people named Hanchett—a name not in the *Dictionary of National Biography*. The most conspicuous thing in the church was a circular frame over an arch, enclosing the inscription in large letters: "This church was repair'd 1820. Henry Chambers and John Hill, Churchwardens." Much smaller letters below said: "Fear God and honour the King."

Leaving Ickleton by its chief street, Abbey Street, I entered an open country rising on all sides. I took the south-westerly road towards Elmdon, and then a right-hand turning out of that which went in a straight line to Ickleton Granges. This is probably a new country road, with hedges and only the narrowest of green strips beside it: it is not the Icknield Way. The old road possibly ran along the gently rising ploughland half-way up it, past Rectory Farm. There is still a footpath from near Abbey Farm and the Priory remains to Rectory Farm, which may represent the course of the Icknield Way, continued by a broken line of thorns reaching almost to Ickleton Granges fifty or a hundred yards north-west of the present road. Past the Granges I turned sharp to the right along a drove coming through the corn from Littlebury and Saffron Walden. At a turning on the left to Redland's Hall this road became a county boundary, and I went uphill to the corner of a copse, where it made another bend westward. At the bend there was a triangle of turf upon the right, so that the right-hand bank, which lies beyond this turf, suggested a road coming from the east, that is to say from Rectory Farm and Ickleton Priory. The road was now well up above the land to its right, and I could see the straight ridge near Cambridge which carries the Mare Way. On the other hand were the gentle Anthony Hill and Clay Hill, and in front the high land above Royston and its straight bars of wood. The road was making almost due west for Royston. It went between corn, clover, or new-ploughed land; white bryony

Approaching Royston.

grew in its low hedges, and even sprawled over the dusty, rabbity mound by the wayside; and it had grass borders of its own width. At first it was rough, but hard and white. Soon it became practically a green road, and then wholly so, but level and rideable. In one place it was lined by lime trees; in others all was elder flower, wild rose, and lady's slipper, and the chatter of young birds. Beyond the road to Dottrell Hall and the lovely group of sycamore and hornbeams at the crossing, it was much worn again. It was a farm road used only by waggons and men between field and field, or at most between farm and farm. It might have seemed no more than a series, four miles long, of consecutive cart tracks, rarely with a hedge on both sides, between it and the cultivated land. It gave a sense of privacy and freedom combined. At a cottage, one of two that had once been a single farm, and still had a thatched shed and a weedy yard, I knocked to ask for water.

A huge wheel and windlass and a seven-gallon tub stood above a well in the yard. A wild-looking cat bounded through the window of one of the cottages which seemed to be empty. The other might also have been empty, in spite of its dirty muslin curtain, for I knocked long and no one came. Just as I was turning to get water for myself a human being with black hair and wild eyes looked out of an upper window and hailed me with a kind of scream. As she was not half dressed, I told her to leave me to look after myself. The well seemed bottomless, but I had the seven gallons of dark, bright water up on the edge by the time my hostess appeared with a dirty cup. She was a thin, hawk-faced woman, bare and brown to the breast, and with glittering blue eyes, and in her upper jaw three strong teeth. She was dressed in black rags. She shaded her eyes to look at me, as if I were half a mile away.

"You're thin, boy," she said, "like me."

"Yes."

A pause.

"Are you middling well off?"

"Yes, middling. Are you?"

"Oh, middling; but times are hard."

"They are."

She looked extraordinarily sad, and I said:—

"Still, we shall have a few years to wait for the workhouse."

"Have to wait a few years!" she repeated, very serious, though smiling. "Have you come from Royston?"

"No; Newmarket."

"Newmarket. Are you going far?"

"To Odsey, between Royston and Baldock."

"It's a long way. You're thin, boy."

"Food doesn't nourish me. Men cannot live on bread only, not even brown bread made at home."

"No."

"Now in the moon, perhaps, I should get fat."

"Perhaps indeed, and I too. But look at the moon. You give me the horrors. You couldn't live *there*."

It was a thin three-quarters of a circle in a hot sky.

"But," I said, "I should like to try."

"Would you?"

"Yes, provided I were someone different. For, as for me, this is no doubt the best of all possible worlds."

"Better than the moon?"

"Yes, better than the moon; and there is nothing better in it than your well water, missus. Good afternoon."

Framed clearly against her solitary pink-washed cottage, she stared after me, shading her eyes.

Two or three times along these four miles of road I saw a square of trees protecting a farm or "grange," most of the villages having a grange out in the open country named after them, as Duxford Grange, Ickleton Grange, Chrishall Grange, Heydon Grange. But on the road itself there were no houses except Noon's Folly and one called Shapens, not even at the crossings of more important roads. For the most part it kept level: where it had to dip slightly after the turn to Great Chishall it was worn several feet deep, but this was exceptional. Beyond that it was worn unevenly into two parallel tracks between hedges with beech trees and elders. To the right the pleasant tree-crowned rise of Goffer's Knoll stood up on the other side of the main Newmarket and Royston road, now fast nearing my road. Past Noon's Folly Farm the road had a narrow and embanked course, but parallel with it a depression seamed by paths and cart tracks. Here and for some way past—from half-way between Noon's Folly and the Barley road—the way is a boundary between Cambridgeshire and Hertfordshire. I had not been out of Cambridgeshire since I left Suffolk at the Kennett bridge.

Half a mile west of Noon's Folly the main road

Icknield Way, crossing Ermine Street.

reached my road, and, turning west instead of south-west, made use of its course for the two miles into Royston. For most of the two miles this piece of road, exactly continuing my old way, had broad green edges, and on the left hand, beeches. Coming to a rise it was cut through the ridge and embanked again below. It went straight through the big village or little town of Royston, where it crossed Ermine Street, and took the name of Baldock Street from the town ahead. As it was market day everyone was driving out of Royston with his trap full of chickens and parcels of all kinds, not to speak of wife and children. This was my first real chance of a lift. For between Ickleton and the Royston road only farm waggons went, and they were all in the hayfields ; and only motor-cars travelled the road from Newmarket, all passing me as if I needed nothing but more dust to fill eyes, mouth, nose, ears, shoes, and spirit. I have never been offered a lift by a stranger in a motor-car, but friends of mine have told me they have heard of others who have. With the increase of dust and heat the likelihood of a merciful motorist becomes less, because dust and heat do not produce the appearance desirable in a motorist's companion ; in fact, by the end of the day, or of the week, especially if he has forgotten to shave, or has always arrived in a town after shop-shutting, the wayfarer runs the risk of being called "mate" by the baker's man who refuses to let him ride. "Mate" sounds like liberty, equality, and fraternity, but it can really be contemptuous pity. It is no better than "my man" from a gentleman, or "unfortunate sister" from a lady, or "my friend" from a Nonconformist minister. In London it may be different, and I should say that a navvy would use it in a friendly manner. But from the Wallingford baker's man on a country round it means "Poor ——," perhaps even "Dirty ——." By this time essays on walking and walking tours begin to wear very thin. You pitch Stevenson at any rate over the hedge, and cannot find a place suitable for —— and ——. Borrow is safe, but then, he got really tired, and did not regard walking as an amusement. I have no doubt that he had learned to stick out his under-lip at the end of some of his marches.

Nevertheless, stumping along on a shoeful of blisters is not bad when you are out of Royston and have Pen Hills upon your left; low, insignificant, restful stretches upon your right; and Odsey before you in the cool of evening. For some distance there was no hedge on the left side of the road beyond the town, and the turf, marked for many yards with tracks made before metalling, rose up to considerable swells of chalk cloven sometimes gently and sometimes abruptly into coombes, some smooth as lawns, some beautiful with trees. Tumuli were scattered over this smoothest sward, and down from the ridge of the high land came deep, curving trackways. At Odsey beyond they have found with Samian pottery the shin bones of men who ran instead of walking. People were walking for pleasure on the grass up above, and children were laughing somewhere near but out of sight.

It was one of those delicious cool ends to perfect days which give a man the feeling of having accomplished something, but by no means compel him to inquire what. The road still possessed the hills even when it was enclosed on both sides, for it kept broad margins, the hedges were low between it and the grass or corn land, and it mounted higher and higher. They were the gentlest of chalk hills crested with trees—Thrift Hill, Gallows Hill, Crouch Hill, Pott's Hill, Rain Hill, Wheat Hill, Windmill Hill, and Weston Hills—and at their highest points there were villages, like Therfield, Kelshall, Sandon, Wallington, Clothall, Weston. I had still four or five miles to walk at the feet of these hills, through a silence undisturbed by the few market carts at long intervals. I am glad now that I walked them. It seems to me now that my purely physical discomfort intensified the taste of the evening's beauty, as it certainly made sweeter the perfection of enjoyment which I imagine possible at such an hour and in such a place. The road was serpentining very little, but enough to conceal from me for a long time the chief wayside marks ahead, as well as my destination. I could always see about a quarter of a mile before me, and there the white ribbon disappeared among trees. And this quarter-mile was agreeable in itself, and always suggesting something better beyond, though itself a sufficient end, if need were. Moreover, I was looking out for a house which I had never seen or heard described. A wood-pigeon came sloping down from the far sky with fewer and fewer wing strokes and longer and longer glidings upon half-closed wings as it drew near its home tree. It disappeared; another flew in sight and slanted downward with the same "folding-in" motion; and then another. The air was silent and still, the road was empty. The birds coming home to the quiet earth seemed visitors from another world. They seemed to bring something out of the sky down to this world, and the house and garden where I stayed at last were full of this something. I heard rooks among the tall beeches of just such a house as I knew I ought to have been able to imagine, with the help of the long white road and the gentle hills, the tall trees, the rooks, and the evening. There were flowers and lawns, beeches and sycamores, belonging to three centuries, perhaps more, and stately but plain red brick of the same date, and likely to endure for a yet longer period, if not by its own soundness, then by its hold upon the fantasy of men who build nothing like it.

CHAPTER V

THIRD DAY—ODSEY TO EDLESBOROUGH, BY BALDOCK, LETCHWORTH, ICKLEFORD, LEAGRAVE, AND DUNSTABLE

THE rooks had been talking in my sleep much too long before I started next day. Their voices and the blazing window-blind described the morning for me before I stirred. I could see and feel it all; and if I could write it down as I saw and felt it this would be a good book and no mistake. The long grasses were dewy cool, the trees lightly rustling and full of shadow, the sky of so soft a greyness that it seemed an impossible palace for a sun so gorgeous. The thrushes sang, and seeing a perfect crimson strawberry, I picked it, and found that it was as hot as a strawberry can be, and therefore at its sweetest and richest.

Winding a little more than before, and still closely attended on its right by the Great Northern Railway, the road entered Baldock, or rather it approached that town, and then, refusing to be a main road any longer, turned off before the Toll Bar Inn to the right. Thus it dipped into the northern edge of the town close to the railway and the station, as a long, sordid lane called Bygrave Lane or Deadman's Lane, past the gasworks, past the "Stag," the "Swan," and the "Black Eagle" in a row. This was the abode of the "Sand Boys," who sold

Deadman's Lane, Baldock.

sand all over the country, and bought bones and rabbit skins. It is also the reputed scene of the death of Gypsy Smith's wife and his own conversion. Past the nobly named public-houses the narrow street became a lane. rutted and half green, and edged on the left with nettles of wondrous height and density. The railway was closer and closer on the right ; on the left was a new cemetery behind tall railings. At length the railway passed under the road. I was now again between high, extravagant hedges of thorn and wild roses. The road was wider, but rough, half green and half rutted, and in places divided into two by a thicket of blackthorn standing in the midst. A nightingale was singing among the roses above some old chalk pits.

After a road from a level crossing had come in on the left, I kept straight on along the right side of a hedge dividing the railway from a big field, and past the left edge of a shallow chalk pit. There was no road here, but several tracks went through the long grass, and mistake was impossible. On the right two paths went off to some of the new houses of the Letchworth Garden City, and to a building gigantically labelled "IDRIS." This was, I suppose, the temple of this city's god, though the name, except as the Welsh equivalent for Arthur, was unknown to me. They say now that Arthur was a solar hero, and when in doubt men might do worse than to worship the sun, if they could discover how. At Letchworth they were endeavouring to do so. The sun was not benign or even merciful in return for these efforts. He responded by telling the truth with his most brilliant beams, so that the city resembled a caravan of bathing machines, except that there was no sea and the machines could not conveniently be moved.

At the end of the big field I crossed a new road and entered among the elders and thorn trees of the edge of Norton Common. Here there were several parallel paths, and on the left behind a hedge was a garden-city street called "Icknield Way." This represented the line of the road, but whether this or the path on the other side of the hedge was more on the old course I cannot say. Past the houses "Icknield Way" ceased to be a road fit for perambulators and became a rough track, chiefly used for carrying building materials. It followed along a hedge and past a sand pit, in one place a little hollowed out. It was miserable with the rank grass of newly "developed" districts. After a road came in from under the railway on the left, it began to curve away north and leave the railway. Once more it was between hedges; but with all its vicissitudes it had remained a parish boundary all the way from Slip Inn Hill near Odsey. It was going uphill, and presently I could see not only the corn, sainfoin, and houses growing round about, but in the south-west the line of hedged and wooded hills above Ippollitts, Offley, and Pirton. Letchworth was still in sight, like so many wounds on the earth and so much sticking-plaster. But, though behind me, it was fascinating, like all these raw settlements. It is a curious pleasure to see them besieged by docks and nettles, and, as sometimes happens, quietly overcome by docks and nettles. They look new until suddenly they are unvenerably old. Letchworth may turn out to be an exception, but as I hurried through it, some back gardens, some forlorn new roads, and the tune of "She's off with the

The Ford, Ickleford.

wraggle-taggle gipsies, oh!" sent my thoughts mysteriously but irresistibly to the desolate new-old settlements I have known.

At the hill-top the road made westward, a shady hedge on the left, sunny sainfoin on the right, and arrived at Wilbury Camp. The north side of the camp touched the Bedfordshire border. The high, irregular earth walls overgrown with thorn trees made an uneven and much delved enclosure, where it was impossible to distinguish gravel pit from camp, and through this hollow and among its thorns went the path I took instead of along the southern hedge and wall, which appears to be the canonical Icknield Way and the parish boundary. Across it goes the hard road coming from Brook End over Wilbury Hill and down to Walsworth. On the other side of this road it was a wide, many-tracked, green way, winding through open corn-land down to the trees of Ickleford; and on its left, at the convenient distance of two miles, the tower and roof clusters and trees of Hitchin replaced the spots of Letchworth. There were hedges with elms for the mowers to rest under, and on the right was the white wall of a chalk pit, with roses and privet overhanging, and black bryony and elder growing below. The way descended to be crossed by two lines of railway a few yards apart. Between the two it was grassy and elm-shaded. Beyond the second the road forded the River Hiz, and even waded in it for thirty yards or so. Ickleford village had a green with chestnut trees, a "Green Man" and an "Old George," and a church wall decorated regularly all over with an incised design of saws, swords, handcuffs, crowns, etc. The road passed St. Catherine's Church and the

"Green Man" on its right, and went out of Ickleford at "Ickleford Gate" on the Hitchin road. This it crossed and went against the course of the River

Ickleford Church.

Oughton, which flowed and turned a mill a little below upon the left. At first it was a green-edged road of good surface, with hedges and telegraph posts, making for the downs, for Telegraph Hill, Deacon Hill, and Tingley Wood, between Pirton and Lilley. But at the mill, its modern use gone, the road was once more a broad, green way dipping with many ruts down among the willowy buttercup meads of the Oughton. Doves cooed; blackcaps poured out their cool, fiery wine of melody; and the cattle meditated about nothing under the elms. The road was rising again, crossed the Pirton and Hitchin road at Punch's Cross, and entered through the gate of an oat-field, travelling along its hedge and out by another gate. At Punch's Cross it became a parish boundary, which it ceased to be at the River Hiz. Up on the right above the ploughland lay Tingley Wood and a beech clump. On the left charlock and corn divided by elms and hedges extended to a wall of low wooded hills. Out of the field the way was a green-hedged lane entered under the rustling welcome of beech trees. Then it became part of the main road from Barton-in-the-Clay to Hitchin, and at the turning southward to Offley a boundary between Bedfordshire and Hertfordshire. This part of the road was partly on a terrace along the side of a hill sloping to the south, and there were roses and traveller's joy buds in the hedges. At one point the land on the left had apparently been too steep to enclose at its lower side, and the hedge was at the top of this steep portion, which was therefore a broad, rough triangle of open turf beside the road. Beyond this the way had good grass banks or level margins with hazel and thorn hedges, and ash or elm trees above them. It was drawing near to a rough and thorny chalk hill called Deacon Hill, and as it was bent on climbing over this range, the modern road left it, and, going westward, avoided the heights above three hundred feet. The Icknield Way took a

On Telegraph Hill.

south-westerly course, and mounted steeply up as a green, almost rutless lane between high hedges. It was green and even as soon as it left the hard road, and now for the first time made a real bold ascent of the chalk. It looked more like a part of the Ridgeway, but for the high hedges, than the unadventurous road that I travelled from Thetford. There were daisies all over it, and roses hung upon either side. Nearing the hill-top it narrowed, and had steep banks on the left with brambles and thorns over them. But right to the top it kept those high hedges. Below on the right lay a neat, green-hedged vale and a long, gentle slope covered with woods or horizontal lines of trees up to a straight low ridge. Telegraph Hill, which the road crossed, is over six hundred feet high. It is difficult to understand why it should make this climb instead of circumventing the hill by a sharp curve southward. It never again does such a thing or rises to such an altitude. At the summit a green ridgeway leaves it. It was easy to glide into this and wind with it to Lilley Hoo and Lilley. The track was a hedgeless, green band among thistles and isolated thorns, glittering dark hollies, and ash trees. Here and there the sheep rested in the shade of a little bramble and thorn thicket, where an oak or ash buried its trunk, and roses climbed. The clear, high tinkling of the bells on still wandering sheep was almost as gay as if the bells were on dancers' feet. The turf on the track was the finest, and was bounded by a tussocky line on one side, if not both. And so it serpentined on the high, flat back of the hills, always among old, isolated thorns or small, clear-cut thickets.

But this was not the Icknield Way, which went straight over Telegraph Hill, and steeply and deeply worn, down to a green lane on the other side, where it was joined on the left by another track descending from a little tumulus with two thorns on it. The green lane winding south-westward was broad, but the spread of the beeches on its left side was broader and roofed it wholly; the turf was better when this line of trees came to an end. Suddenly a chalk pit on the left narrowed it, and this narrowness had been continued on, and used for wheat as far as the next turning. Thenceforward it widened, and had rough hedges of elder and nettles, holly and ash, between it and the undulating corn. In front bulked the smooth ridge of Galley Hill. Past the turning to Offley there were four or five tracks parallel but on different levels, with an embanked one in the centre. Soon it was again on the turf of the Downs, curving around the right base of Galley Hill, the open land on the left, hedges and fields on the right; past the hill there were two hedges and ploughed land on either hand. Hereby was the entrance into Bedfordshire. Then it came almost at right angles to the straight mound of Dray's Ditches, but turned to the right along it, followed by the parish boundary into the Luton and Bedford road. If, instead of going alongside the ditches, I had gone straight ahead upon the line of the way, I should have struck this road at the sixteenth milestone, and at the opposite turning to Leagrave which I actually took. The boundary, on the other hand, went on over the main road towards Houghton. The road down to Leagrave was an ordinary hedged road with narrow, green edges. After passing a little copse on the left I turned on the same side, by an ash a century old, into a broad green track to Limbury. It had hedges, but that on the left strayed away round a huge rushy space. Beyond this was the clean orange wall of a sand pit, and then a green field, and then the tree-tops, and the crowd of roofs and the tall chimneys of Luton, and in the midst a tower above all the rest. But the hedge returned and the way narrowed, and it had to cross Leagrave Marsh and the tiny Lea. There was a choice of road or path. Entering the brand-new, jerry-built, slated cages of combined Limbury and Leagrave Marsh, I turned to the right along Limbury Road, and found on my left the Icknield Way, giving its name to an estate and a new street.

Leagrave Marsh was evidently a pleasant little ford village before it became what it now seems to be—a safety-valve for Luton. The harsh, new streets led me to a rushy common threaded by the Lea, and bounded on my side by a road that crossed the stream with a bridge. At one side of the bridge the "Three Horse Shoes" faced over the common and along the water; ponies, traps, and dogs were clustered at the door in the sun. Their owners were either inside, getting hot, or lying on the grass over the way. But one driver was taking his horse and trap through the stream close to the bridge; and the whipped foam was shining and the spokes flashing. Some boys were paddling a little way above; and above them the village geese were nibbling among the rush tufts. In and out among horses and traps, men, dogs, boys, and geese, the martins were flying.

The Icknield Way went between the new houses and across the Midland Railway and so down a field rotten-ripe for building into Oak Road, which leads from old Leagrave into the Luton and Dunstable road. This road interrupted my way, which went formerly as a footpath straight across it and into the main road a little west of the Half-way House, between Dunstable and Luton. This path was ploughed up and its course only in part noticeable among the crops. The Luton and Dunstable road now looked like a river and the footpath a tiny brooklet whose drying up made no difference to the main stream. But in Robert Morden's map of 1695 the "Icnal Way" is a clear, good road past Leagrave and into Dunstable, while the road to that town from Luton is parallel with the "Icnal Way," and apparently the same as the road and footpath running half a mile south of the present road and just south of the Hatfield, Luton, and Dunstable branch of the Great Northern line. This main road was a substantial, broad, straightforward highway running along level ground and parallel to the downs on its left. There were a few beeches in its low hedges, and the margins of grass were of the ordinary width and rich in dust. Three or four miles of the clear hills, here and there crowned by trees, curved alongside and then slightly across my course. Opposite the turning to Houghton the lime works of Blow's Down broke the green wall with white.

As I entered Dunstable there was already a touch of night in the light, and it fell with a sad blessing upon the low-towered church and the sheep grazing

Dunstable Downs.

in the churchyard up above the road on my left. The crossing of the Icknield Way and Watling Street makes Dunstable. Watling Street was wider and had the town hall, the post office, the bigger shops, and the chief inns. The Icknield Way, known first as Church Street, then as West Street, was the more rustic, humble, and informal, and beyond the crossing it had trees by its side; and this seemed natural and just. It had become thoroughly suburban before leaving the town and coming to the smooth high downs on the left, where children were playing and girls walking about above a field of barley and charlock beside the road. On my right there was a wide border of level down turf and no hedge between it and the corn. The downs, or I should say the Chiltern Hills, proceeded majestically southward, but six or seven miles away advanced somewhat to the east, half clothed in woods, until the bare Beacon Hill stopped steep and abrupt above a high plateau of cornland which fell away into a broad, wooded lowland on my right. Round this Beacon I could see that my road would bend; I thought I could see the ledge it must follow. In that lower land on my right there were several rises. Such was the smooth, easy sweep of Toternhoe, close to Luton; such the wooded heave upon which rose the dark, noble tower of Edlesborough Church; and such the terraced hill near Edlesborough, with a few thorns on the slopes between the terraces, and at its foot a long, neat orchard of late plums or "prunes." The broad, wayside strip on the right hand sometimes showed the old course of my way much below the level of the present road; and after Well Head this lower course was beyond and below the modern hedge. On the left, at Well Head, I noticed a little hill on this side of the main ridge very prettily terraced, with thorns on the slopes between the terraces. At Well Head a deep, smooth-sided cleft winds away to Dolittle Mill, with the first waters of the Ouse. A similar cleft a mile or so beyond, at the Cross Waters, close to the entrance into Buckinghamshire, carries water to the mills of Eaton Bray. As I came out of Dunstable I thought there could be nothing there equal to the sweep of the downs before me, ending in the wooded Ivinghoe Hills and the Beacon. But when I had gone more than half-way towards the end of the sweep I looked back and saw that the downs behind me were equal to those I was approaching, and even advanced a little out of the straight like the others, ending also in a promontory above Dunstable. The air was now still and the earth growing dark and already very quiet. But the sky was light and its clouds of utmost whiteness were very wildly and even fiercely shaped, so that it seemed the playground of powerful and wanton spirits knowing nothing of earth. And this dark earth appeared a small though also a kingly and brave place in comparison with the infinite heavens now so joyous and so bright and out of reach. I was glad to be there, but I fell in with a philosopher who seemed to be equally moved yet could not decide whether his condition was to be described as happiness or melancholy. He talked about himself. He was a lean, indefinite man; half his life lay behind him like a corpse, so he said, and half was before him like a ghost. He told me of just such another evening as this and just such another doubt as to whether it was to be put down to the account of

Beacon Hill, Ivinghoe.

happiness or melancholy. He said that he had been digging all day in a heavy soil, often jarring the fork against immovable flints, lifting more often than not a weight of clay only just short of the limit of his strength. He had thought and thought until his brain could do nothing but remain aware of dull misery and the violent shocks of the hard work. But his eyes saw the sun go down with a brief pomp of crimson soon covered up by funereal drifts, and these in their turn give way to a soft blue, full of whitest stars and without one cloud. They saw the far hills once more take on their night look of serene and desolate vastness, and felt the meadows of the valley become dark and uncertain, the woods much duller but distinct. The woods immediately below him on the hill-side thickened and appeared more wild and impossible ; the road winding up between them like a long curl of smoke was wholly concealed. Slowly the solid world was whittled away. The lights of the small town half-way across the valley, towards the hills, came out.

As an owl in the woods announced the triumph of night with one large, clear note, he straightened himself slowly and painfully among the clods. It would have been easier to continue his toil than to do this, but he did it, and then cleaned the prongs of his upright fork with the toe of his boot, prolonging the action as if he either hoped to arrive now at some significant conclusion with its help or feared the next step that had to be taken. When he could no longer clean the prongs he raised his head and looked out beyond the woods over the valley to the far hills. The quiet, the magnitude of space, the noble lines of the range a little strengthened his spirit. He remained still. The surface of his hands was dry to brittleness; he was stiff and yet unsatisfied with the result of his labour; he felt the dulness of his eyes; and no thing or person in the world or out of it came into his mind with any conscious delight or quickness; yet he still looked along the ridges of the hills from one end to the other, from star to star, without a thought save the sleeping, underlying one that he was growing old.

A motor-car climbed nervously up the invisible hill-road, the lamps of it darting across a hundred little spaces between one tree and another of the vague woods. It left the silence stronger than ever.

The man leaned with his chest upon his hands, which were upon the handle of his fork. Only a few years ago—either three or four—he could not have ascertained by any searching of memory—he had been young, and treated with contempt or with pitiful kindness by those of more years. But now he had come by unknown ways to feel that he differed from mature men, not by anything positive that could be called youth, but only by some undefinable lack which condemned him to a kind of overblown immaturity. Thus when he consciously or unconsciously demanded a concession such as might be due to youth for some act or attitude, he met, in the individual or in society in some corporate form or other, a blankness or positive severity at which he recoiled with open but as yet uncertainly comprehending eyes. Of young men he was now sometimes jealous ; of middle-aged men afraid and no longer defiant. Towards the contemporaries with whom he had shared thought and experience for some years he felt jealousy, if he seemed to have outstripped them in the unwilling race; fear, if it was himself that lagged; and towards only one or two a fair and easy freedom, and that only intermittently. Therefore no more destitute and solitary man looked that night on the stars. Yet they were as bright and the hills under them as noble as those we saw to-day on the road from Dunstable.

Suddenly he awakened and thrilled to the sound of a woman's voice singing alone somewhere away from where he stood. He forgot who and where he was. He was no longer weary and muddied by self-supporting thoughts. His imagination went out of him and grasped each note simply and boldly. Where there had been nothing, there the liquid voice mounted in its beautiful, unseen form amidst the darkness. The singer was among the dark trees, probably in the climbing road to one side of him ; the curve of that ascent, always a thing of simplicity and nobleness, was now glorious, romantic as it soared out of the valley to the clear heights.

Either the singer was walking slowly up or she was riding, but no footfall or turn of wheel was to be heard. It was a powerful voice, confident and without care. It leapt up with a wild, indolent flight, for one short verse of indistinguishable words, in a melody exulting in the wildness of love and pride of youth, and then fell upon silence. That silence bore its part also.

But the listener had no sooner lost the first joy over the insurrection of melody, begun to consider—whilst waiting breathless for its return—who she might be, what she was doing now, whether a lover was walking beside her, when she sang again, higher up the road. The first note rose up to the highest stars, clear and fresh and having a power like light over the gloom. Other notes hovered after it at the same height, and then with one swoop as of an eagle fell to the earth and silence before even a verse was finished. A low laugh drawn out very long an instant afterwards confirmed the first impression of the singer's ease and joyousness. The man could see her neck lifted eagerly and her eyes flashing towards the lover or towards the stars, her lips parted, her breast heaving with deep draughts of the night and passion, her feet pacing with languid strength. He himself stood still as any tree in the ebb of the wind.

Oh, for a horse to ride furiously, for a ship to sail, for the wings of an eagle, for the lance of a warrior or a standard streaming to conquest, for a man's strength to dare and endure, for a woman's beauty to surrender, for a singer's fountain of precious tones, for a poet's pen!

He trembled and listened. The silence was unbroken; not a footstep or whisper was to be extracted from it by his eager and praying ear. He shivered in the cold. The last dead leaves shook upon the beeches, but the silence out there in that world still remained. She was walking or she was in her lover's arms, for aught he knew. No sound came up to him where he stood eager and forlorn until he knew that she must be gone away for ever, like his lyric desires, and he went into his house and it was dark and still and inconceivably empty.

As I turned into the inn and left him he was inclined either to put down that evening half to happiness and half to melancholy, or to cross out one or other of those headings as being in his case tautological.

The landlady at my inn was the first that ever told me outright, at once, and without being asked, what she charged for a bed, and as the sum was reasonable I was doubly pleased. She was a jaunty, probably childless London woman not far from forty, who referred to her husband as "my sweetheart." She had a skittish, falsetto laugh, whether she was talking to me about their old horse John and all his merits, or to the labourers about such and such a "sweet old house" in the neighbourhood. They were speaking of the coronation bonfire that was building on the Beacon Hill, and she became important and full of reminiscences of the Hampstead Heath bonfire, and, thereanent, the Spaniards, Vale of Health, and so on. She hovered between them and me, anxious to tell me that much as she liked a country life she missed the gas and the bathroom of a London house. Now and then she left us all, to talk to the parrot in a loud voice intended for mankind as well as Polly. Her "sweetheart" turned out to be a little active man, superficially jaunty but silent and brooding and hanging down his head. He was sandy-haired with dull, restless, blue eyes, and had not recently been shaved. His turned-out feet stepped quickly hither and thither. He was dressed anyhow and as if he slept in his clothes to ensure a fit; a white scarf was tied round his neck and his trousers were turned up. He carried a cigarette either in the corner of his mouth or behind his ear. He was one of those creatures provided by an almighty providence for attending on that "noble animal" (such he called it) the horse; but this did not prevent him from calling his own horse John "old son." He never carried a whip, because, he said, he did not believe in hurting "dumb animals." A man who knows horses well is equally at home in town or country, and though this man was as full-blooded a Cockney as his wife, he was, like her, contented with his three or four years of country solitude; it was, he said, a "happy life, yes, a happy life," better than what we had learnt to call the "bustle and confusion" of London. I asked him about the Icknield Way, which he knew by that name, and he told me that it was a Roman road and that he had heard a man could walk on it for twelve months and come back to the same place again. What that place was he did not say; probably he meant any place and imagined that the road made a circuit of this island or belike of the great globe itself. There could be no better landlord and landlady of a small wayside inn with one horse, one trap, and one spare bed. The bed was clean and comfortable, and I fell asleep in it while the stone-curlews were piping on the downs and a pair of country wheels were rolling by, late and slow.

CHAPTER VI

FOURTH DAY—EDLESBOROUGH TO STREATLEY, ON THE UPPER ICKNIELD WAY, BY WENDOVER, KIMBLE, WHITELEAF, GIPSIES' CORNER, IPSDEN, AND CLEEVE

"FIVE o'clock, sir," said the Cockney at my door next morning, and I looked out to see a hot day slowly and certainly preparing in mist and silence. There was nobody in the fields. The hay-waggon stood by the rick where it had arrived too late to be unloaded last night. To one bred in a town this kind of silence and solitariness perhaps always remains impressive. We see no man, no smoke, and hear no voice of man or beast or machinery, and straightway the mind recalls very early mornings when London has lain silent but for the cooing of pigeons. That silence of so many things that can and will make sounds gives some of its prestige to the country silence of very quiet things. Therefore when I have looked out of a strange window for the first time and seen nothing move but leaves on the earth and clouds in the sky, I have often for a moment felt as if it were dawn and have slipped into a mood of dawn ; it might be possible on a cloudy day and in a new country to be deceived thus even at noon. Thus the innocence of silent London is transferred to the downs, the woods, the vacant fields, and the road without a wheel or a foot upon it for miles and miles.

I had about forty miles to cover before the end of the daylight, so I had to help myself by driving with my host and his "old son" John. I was now thoroughly foot-sore. One foot was particularly bad, and in trying to save it I used different muscles in the leg, which were quickly tired. Then, to help myself, I had leaned heavily on my stick at every step and so brought arm and shoulder to a state of discomfort, if not pain. Finally, the stick was unsuitable for its purpose and sorely afflicted the palm of the hand that grasped it. I had carried the stick for many single days of walking and liked it. For it was a tapered oak sapling cut in the Weald and virtually straight because its slightly spiral curves counteracted one another. But it had almost no handle, and so drove itself into one small portion of the palm when leaned on. It had also in the winter shown itself hard to retain in the hand when a few inches of it were in mud. Nevertheless, it was so nicely balanced and being oak so likely to last a lifetime that, for six years, I put up with its faults, and now, having been in my company for so many miles in a splendid June, it has a fresh hold upon me. Also I am not certain that any other handle, a larger and rounder knob or a stout natural crook, would have been much better in a hand not made of iron. Perhaps a really long staff grasped some way from its upper end would be right. But there is something too majestic, patriarchal even, about such a staff. A man would have to build up his life round about it if it had been deliberately adopted. And gradually he would become a celebrity. Of course, if he had an inclination towards such a staff, as the natural and accredited form among pedestrians, there would be an end of the matter, but that is not very likely in a town-bred Englishman. He must meditate upon what might have been, and be content to make five shillings out of his meditation, if he is a journalist.

It was a pleasure to drive with Mr. Willcocks. He became quite silent apart from civility. He evidently understood the horse, and the horse him, in the mutual manner usually expected from a legal monogamous union. If he had sat on the horse's back the combination would have been nothing like a centaur. But with one between the shafts and the other holding the reins they were one spirit in two bodies.

As we began to curve round the foot of the Ivinghoe Hills, which were on our left, we passed another but larger deep cleft, like those at Well Head and Cross Waters, below the road, upon our right, called Coombe Hole. There was another Coombe a mile to the south ; but before this I had not met the name (hardly the thing, except on the west of Royston) since I left Thetford. We went close under the steep slope of Beacon Hill which was tipped with a tumulus and scored upon its flanks by many old descending trackways. Away to the right there was no land so high as our road—about five hundred feet; the hill-tops were half as high again—for farther than eye could see; and to all this low land of dairy and garden the road was a boundary. We were approaching the place where the Icknield Way is said to divide into two parallel courses. A road from Leighton Buzzard strikes athwart the course and following along this to the left for half a mile you turn to the right into the "Upper Icknield Way"; following it to the right you reach Ivinghoe and there turn to the left into the "Lower Icknield Way." We were going to take the Upper, so called as being higher up the slope of the land. Just before the Leighton Buzzard road we passed on our left a long cleft, smooth and flat-bottomed, with horses feeding in it, and hereabouts the old course or part of its original width was clear over the left-hand hedge. On our right was a high bank round which went the road to Ivinghoe, and this bank would explain the sharp turn. Originally it may well have been that the road forked, the Lower going past the old windmill straight ahead and so to Pitstone Green and missing Ivinghoe; the Upper going with it to the old windmill and there diverging to the left past Pitstone Church and out into the road now marked "Upper Icknield Way" at Folly Farm. Along this road there was a border of close grass; chestnuts or sycamores of about thirty years stood up here and there in the hedge, and over it I saw Ivinghoe Church tower and the silly spire, short and sharp, on top of it, the misty woods behind, and the protuberance of Southend Hill, having its sides carved into thorny terraces, "linces" or "linchetts" ; the Pitstone Church tower and an elm throned on a rise together, and the broad wooded valley beyond. The air was sweet now with roses, now with yellow bedstraw. Larks sang, and a yellowhammer that forgot the end of its song, and once a blackbird. I had left behind the Ivinghoe Hills, but Pitstone Hill, their successor, was of the same brood. It was chiefly bare, and its flanks much-modelled as well as scarred by a slanting trackway. The land between the foot of it and the road was carved with the utmost ingenuity of which chalk is capable. Once there was a succession of long parallel deep rolls at right angles to the road ; wheat and barley grew on them except in one or two places where the fall was too steep and there were thorns amidst the corn. I saw also several of those natural walls formed by a sudden change of level. These are generally used as divisions between fields. Here there was wheat above and wheat below, and along the bottom of the wall a cart track went between lines of poppies up to the hill. Another such wall, but higher, had beeches on its slope, and it made a fine curve up to its end at the foot of the hill.

Half a mile past the turn to Pitstone Church the way becomes a boundary between Buckinghamshire and Hertfordshire as far as the bridge over the Grand Junction Canal, where I entered Hertfordshire again, leaving it nearly two miles beyond and not far from the junction with Akeman Street. At a dip from Tring wharf the road narrowed and lost its green edges, but regained them on the more level ground. For a little while after the crossing to Tring Church a narrow green track was raised on the right above the road and between it and the hedge. Here there was an elm, and there several, and here an ash; and there was never no charlock. The hills on the left were more and more wooded with beeches; and they curved round so as to lie slightly across our course. On the right lay the broad reservoirs of the canal at the edge of the Vale of Aylesbury.

Now once more the Icknield Way is thrown out of its course for a little way, this time by Akeman Street, a modern road to Aylesbury, the ancient road from this region to Cirencester, which was the junction for Wales, Devon, and Cornwall. It enters Akeman Street a third of a mile east of the thirty-third milestone from London. The Icknield Way was presumably older; it was at least old when Akeman Street was Romanized and came cutting in a straight line across its meanders; and therefore it lost confidence for half a mile and forsook them and took to the Roman straight line until suddenly stumbling upon itself again at one of its meanders further on it returned to its old way. The scene is like the picture of a wandering life interrupted by a year of discipline. The stark telegraph-posts in line seem part of the discipline. Possibly for years, for centuries, the meanders survived, more and more faintly, with the straight line, enclosing a rough and crooked space. This space beside Tring Hill should have been a common for ever; but either it never was or a common award handed it over to the largest mouth. Opposite the milestone it turns out from the main road in its old south-westerly direction, and escapes the telegraph-posts. For some time it was unlike its old self because it

Wendover.

had hardly any grassy margin. It went up and down again and again, and often steeply, and the more hilly a modern road the less likely it is to have wide margins. Near Halton there was a wayside border but little if at all trodden, and not fed down by sheep. A traveller joining the road for a mile or so would have failed to see in it any distant or ancient purpose; it was a winding country lane metalled for modern uses, and by Halton House made polite with firs and laurels. In one place, as we neared Wendover, I saw the old course and its bank and also a hedge beyond the present one. Past Halton Woods the hills recede southward and there is a gap of a mile between steep Boddington Hill and steep Bacombe Hill. Through this gap comes the road from London, Uxbridge, and Amersham to Aylesbury, and the railway with it: at the entrance stands Wendover. Through this long little town of cottages the Icknield Way goes as High Street and Pound Street. We were now close under Bacombe Hill, with its camp and barrow. In front, jutting out and making the road curve west before it could resume its south-west course by a sharp turn south, lay the Coombe Hill and its obelisk, Beacon Hill sprinkled with thorns, and Pulpit Hill. As we climbed the lower slopes of Bacombe Hill I noticed that the roadside green had been dug up and enclosed by a second hedge. Beyond there was a good green margin now on the left and now on the right, and beeches rustled from the hedges; and on both sides grew corn. The road went up and down, coming thus suddenly in sight of Ellesborough Church tower rising pale ahead out of its trees against the clear line of the hills. Past Butler's Cross, where the road from Aylesbury to Hughenden and High Wycombe crosses, the sycamores on the left were beautiful, and so were the beeches, wych-elms and ashes following, and then more sycamores, and still more in a cluster above the high bank by Ellesborough Church. The Chekers Park limes and ashes on the left cooled the road until we came to a pool and Little Kimble

Ellesborough Church.

Church. Then there were more park trees, lime and elm and chestnut, as we went up to the church tower of St. Nicholas at Great Kimble.

At Great Kimble—at the "Bear and Cross"—I got tired of riding at a walk up steep hills and down steep hills, and I took to my feet again.

Just before the second milestone from Princes Risborough, in obedience to my map, I turned to the left and took the right-hand road at a fork. For a quarter mile this was a narrow chalky lane, having at its entrance a sycamore and a thatched cottage, and traveller's joy all over its low hedge; but crossing a road from Great Missenden it became more important, hard and white, with a green border. I climbed up past the "Red Lion" at Whiteleaf, under Whiteleaf Hill, crossed the Wycombe road, and went down a hedged and rutty lane, leaving the spire of Princes Risborough half a mile below on the right. The way was some distance up on a steep slope, and itself in places so steep from side to side that there were two tracks, one two yards above the other. Then it was a broad track of level turf, next a narrow and rough one, the ruts, as near the Horsenden road, mended with lemonade bottles and meat tins. That road also thwarts the Icknield Way, and diverts it half a mile to the left; an old course seemed perhaps to be indicated by a hedge continuing the line of the lane behind. Turning to the right out of this road the Icknield Way was white with green edges, of which one presently became a terrace above the road. Over one railway and under another its level green edges were trimmed with silver-weed; in the hedges there were elms. Past the Bledlow road it was a broad, rough lane, soon green, between hedges; the Chilterns and Wain Hill woods on the left, charlock on the right. It climbed until at the

"Leather Bottle" it reached its highest point since Telegraph Hill, and it had woods both above and below—which rarely happens to it—as it passed

Near the "Leather Bottle."

above the head of a beech-sided coombe having an entrance apparently higher than its back. There were roses in the hedges through these beech woods. The "Leather Bottle" marked the far edge of the wood and the passing of the border into Oxfordshire. Here a steep track slanted down from the hill-top. The road was now narrower, confined by a hedge and bank on the right and the steep wall of the thorn and juniper hill on the left. Presently another deep track came slantwise down from Chinnor Hill towards Bledlow and crossed my way. Beyond this the vale was lovely. At the foot of the hill beyond the railway which followed it was an irregular space of two or three square miles, nearly level but not quite. This was divided into large fields of grass or corn by scarce perceptible hedges or ditches, and crossed by one winding road visible and white at only one of its bends. Along this road and the hedges a very few elms were distributed with indescribable felicity. There would be five at a bend; a row, then a break, and only one or two more; and they made only one long line. One of the fields so divided was lemon-coloured with charlock; on one which was slightly tilted up a few sheep were scattered. Beyond and on either side of this space the trees were thicker, and closed in so that two or three miles away all seemed woodland with an interspace or two, then a grey, dim ridge beyond, all under a grey-folded sky. Above the juniper hill the jackdaws were jacking merrily.

Afterwards the road descended and was a green-hedged line with a narrow ploughed field between it and the edge of the juniper. Above Chinnor it was for a long way almost straight, broad and green, with elms in the left hedge. Here the Chilterns had beeches on the upper slope and dots of juniper below. Suddenly after this straightness the way had to descend a little over undulating ground, and it wriggled ahead confusedly, narrow and without trees in its hedge, widening where a hump was useless, to the ploughland below. In front now stood the clumped Beacon Hill above Lewknor, which was the end of a long curve of hills carrying the woods of Crowell, Kingston, and Aston, woods reaching from the ridge down to the arable in most parts, but with lawny or chalky intervals. At the crossing to Kingston Blount the railway came up to my road and from there went close and parallel for a mile to the station of Aston Rowant. It was here a broad green track at the foot of the slope, though still above everything lying on its right, and leaving the villages at least half a mile on that side. It rounded Beacon Hill, which was capped with a tree-clump and sprinkled with junipers, and went along under Bald Hill and Shirburn Hill, which was wooded. Before crossing the road from Great Marlow and Fingest to Watlington, it wound round a chalk pit and rubbish heap. Then the telegraph-posts joined it, though it was only a green lane in two terraces going under thorny Watlington Hill, and past cornfields sprinkled with charlock and white campion. At one point ten elm trees, one a triple tree, stood out in the middle of the wide green trackway. Beyond the road from Nettlebed the way was white between high, level green banks, and then long grass, thistles, and thorns in a thicket, before coming to the elm-shaded pond where a lane goes up on the left under more elms to Dame Alice Farm. Then it narrowed and widened again among nettles and elder, and a little farther it became a company of four

Icknield Way, near Watlington

parallel grooves paved with the pure down turf, a little silver-weed, and thyme. The undulations of the cornland were bolder now towards Britwell Salome, and in a hollow a roof nestled among elms ;

beyond these were dim, low hills. A line of elm trees, now many deep, now in narrow file, half hid the village of Britwell. Above my road a steam-plough stood idle; the men lay on their faces under the elms; and beyond was their caravan. Crossing the Britwell Salome road I came in sight of the clear heavings of the Sinodun Hills and their clumps of trees, and the dim length of the main downs far past them. Britwell House, looking at its monument and Swyncombe Downs, lay a little to the right. Down the slope of the hill at the north edge of the beeches and firs of Icknield Bank Plantation came a Danish entrenchment.

Emerging from the trees the road was narrow and hard, but sent a green branch southward over Littleworth Hill, and the adjacent land was equally high on both sides, on the left Ewelme Downs, on the right Huntingland. I went along the south side of Ewelme Cow Common, a shallow, irregular hollow of grass, with many thorns and much bird's-foot trefoil in it, bounded on all hands by roads without hedges. I entered the Henley road a little west of the fourteenth milestone from Oxford, and turned along it to the right, and then almost at once to the left at Gipsies' Corner, and so went south, avoiding the road on the right to Crowmarsh Gifford and Wallingford. Here was a new land before me, of sweeping corn, big thatched barns on a low ridge above it, and the main Downs beyond. It was a narrow and low-hedged road that kept away from the low, elmy Thames land on the west. Over the hazels and elders of its

Sinodun Hill

hedgerows climbed roses and bryony. Between Oakley Wood and Coldharbour Farm it made southward, crossing the Nettlebed and Crowmarsh and Nuffield and Crowmarsh roads within a few yards ; the three ways framing a pretty triangular waste of impenetrable thorns, elders, and nettles. Sinodun Hills were always distinct on the right. Then I traversed Grim's Ditch, where it borders the south edge of Foxberry Wood and of a broad, herbless ploughland ; the ditch being on the south side of the bank. In half a mile I crossed another road from Crowmarsh, going south-east. There my way ceased to be a road, but its line was clear along the natural wall of earth between upper and lower fields ; and when there was no more wall, along the strip of rough grass between two stretches of ploughland ; and when that ended, the course of the way was clearly on a terrace with a central path through the long grass and some thorns on the bank to the right of it, between two fields of sainfoin. Ahead, on the left, stood the little solitary church of Ipsden on an east-and-west road from North Stoke which I crossed. Onwards there was a rough, hedgeless road still going south. After the next cross-road to Ipsden the probable line was marked only by a hedge between grass and arable, and even that gave out for the last fifty yards before entering the Mongewell road. Over this road a gap in the hedge might have been used when the road had dwindled to a footpath going to Glebe Farm, which is on a road now largely used to connect Brazier's Park with Goring. I thought I saw the ghost of it coming down to Glebe Farm, though amidst corn. This road to Goring is henceforward along the course of the Icknield Way. It is a hard

Near Cleeve.

and hedgeless road, winding and undulating through corn that rises on either hand to crested ridges. It passed Icknield Farm, crossed the South Stoke and Woodcote road, and went up as Catsbrain Hill to where I saw below me the red roofs and walls of suburban Cleeve and the Berkshire downs, their woods and pastures, beyond. The road dipped, and at the cross-road below was lost in streets and building land. Therefore I turned west along the cross-road, and then south again to Goring, the ford, and Streatley. Goring and Streatley railway station, and the cutting and the new houses have probably covered up where they have not destroyed all traces of the Icknield Way. But there is a Ferry Lane leading down to the towing-path and river, to where there was a ferry before the bridge, and a "Roman" ford over the gravelly bottom before that. On the opposite side Streatley Vicarage and its lawn lie across the probable way, but beyond them a path continuing the line of Ferry Lane goes straight up to the Reading road a quarter mile south of the "Bull." I went into Goring Church and churchyard, and was pleased with the names of "John Lammas" and of "James, Ann, and Ruth Thresher" on tombstones. What clear visages of men and women these call up, each perfect in its way, shorn of the uncertain, vague, or incongruous elements of the living! By a kind of art the mere names in the churchyard sketch the characters. I have seen mere names that suggested as much as those two beautiful verses express which Mr. Walter de la Mare, the author, calls "An Epitaph":—

> Here lies the most beautiful lady,
> Light of step and heart was she;
> I think she was the most beautiful lady
> That ever dwelt in the West Countrie.

But beauty vanishes; beauty passes;
However rare—rare it be;
And when I crumble who will remember
This lady of the West Countrie?

I have seen some that had in them no touch of death except the word, and that did no more than make a rustle and a shadow in the beauty as death does in the same poet's "Three Cherry Trees":—

There were three cherry trees once
Grew in a garden all shady;
And there for delight of so gladsome a sight
Walked a most beautiful lady,
Dreamed a most beautiful lady.

Birds in those branches did sing,
Blackbird and throstle and linnet,
But she walking there was by far the most fair—
Lovelier than all else within it,
Blackbird and throstle and linnet.

But blossoms to berries do come,
All hanging on stalks light and slender,
And one long summer's day charmed that lady away
With vows sweet and merry and tender,
A lover with voice low and tender.

Moss and lichen the green branches deck,
Weeds nod in its paths green and shady;
Yet a light footstep seems there to wander in dreams,
The ghost of that beautiful lady—
That happy and beautiful lady.

As if I had not had enough of it in passing through, I walked out again to Cleeve, and looked at the blocks of red brick houses. Only people with immortal souls could be content with houses like those. For a man without an immortal soul, but a few senses for a substitute, a house like one of these is, to use one poor word instead of a dozen better ones, unsuitable. I have lived in three, and one of them would compete with any house at Cleeve for the title of The Red Brick House.

The Red Brick House was a raw naked building in the county of Kent with a triple bay window to left and right of the front door, and, above these, two large windows and a small one in the middle ; on one side there were no windows, on the other only one very small one low down ; the back was flat and had a door between a large window and a small, and three windows above. The roof was of slate and low-pitched, and there was a stack with three chimney pots at either side of the house, and a single chimney at the back.

The house stood in a level, oblong piece of land cut out of a large field by posts and wire, and separated from the road by a cheap but rustic fence. There were two other buildings of the same species within two hundred yards, all looking across the same road between elm trees to a ploughed field, many hedges, a rise of orchard land, and some heavy wooded hills at the horizon. For the sake of the houses the elms on their side had been felled and taken away. Breaking-down, temporary fowl-houses were littered about two of the gardens, which someone had begun to dig once upon a time, and even to plant and sow ; but there was not a living tree in either of them.

The soil was light. There was no higher ground in the near neighbourhood, and it had therefore been chosen as the site of a square water-tank, imperfectly sequestered among elms close to the house. To the south the view was gentle and perfect, especially when the blossom snow hung in the orchards and the sky was milky soft above the dark woods of the horizon. At the lower edge of these woods stood a white house that was always mysterious, even though it was often seen from a gateway not a hundred yards distant. The Downs flowed to the north. Eastward and westward the last undulations of the Downs could be seen beyond orchards and elms.

The village clustered round a triangular green half a mile away, and in the woods on the slope from the Red Brick House down to the Green, several bigger houses half hid themselves, looking toward the far Downs and the orchard rise. Many other folds of the land held cottages in groups, farm-houses and their spreading dependencies, conical oast-houses, single or sociable, and not a few churches; yet from the Red Brick House only the White House at the wood's edge was visible when the leaves were on the elms of the hedges, on the orchards, and on the oak and beech of the copses and greater woods.

All other houses that I have known, beautiful, plain, dear, hateful, or dull, have been somehow subdued and made spiritual houses in course of time and of memory. The Red Brick House is the only unconquerable one. To this day it remains a body, and dead. Its fires are black grates that burnt coal. Its walls are wall-paper in strips at a certain price. Its garden is still mere hard ground to be dug (and to grow chiefly the inexorable couch-grass). I saw a beautiful spring come into the world from that house: spring passed down the elms on the opposite side of the road, led one morning by a wry-neck screaming loud in the tops of the trees. Pewits came to the ploughed field beyond, and tossed in the sunny wind, as I would have done in such days of March, had I been a bird. Beautiful autumn, beautiful spring, beautiful summer, triumphed round about that building. Many days can I remember from those seasons, a February day, for example—a pale morning after a night of lashing rain, a pale, still morning. The puddles, the ruts of the cartways, the smooth surface of the winding roads, glistened in the brown, ploughed world. The Downs were clear and dark and hard under a silver-clouded blue sky, and far beyond them were the upper ridges of small mountainous clouds of a yellowish and sunlit white. Very sombre were the woods. Each thing was dark or bright; all was fresh and cold. Suddenly a bee twanged through the air to a snowdrop on the south side of the Red Brick House. Inside the house a subtle devil was refusing to let a soul enter into its walls—a subtle but a bodiless and soulless devil, negative and denying. During the nine years since it was built eight families had sojourned in the house, and had not given it a soul; nor had the several intervals of vacancy given it a ghost.

Sometimes death will give a soul to a house. I once saw the soul of a dead man given to a new little house with a verandah. The swifts were racing to and fro between the rows of new houses. They flew just above the level of men's hats, except when they turned with a rapier-like twist up into the air. While they raced they screamed continually shrill screams of a fierce hilarity. There were half a hundred of them all flying as upon the surface of an invisible stream surmounted by a few black, bobbing hats, or, very rarely, an upturned white face; and no part of the streets was for more than a second without a crescent black wing and a shriek. They had taken possession of the town. Under their rush and cry the people in the streets were silent, walking blankly and straight ahead, and all looking old in contrast with the tumultuous and violent youth of the birds. The thought came into my head as I was passing the last of the houses that even so must the birds have been racing and screaming when the Danes harried this way a thousand years ago, and thus went they over the head of Dante in the streets of Florence. In the warriors and in the poet there was a life clearly and mightily akin to that in the bird's throat and wing, but here all was grey, all was dead.

When I came to the bridge leading over the railway to the meadows I stood and watched the birds flying beneath me, above the slowly curving metals; for I could not tire of the wings and voices that ripped the dead air, and I crossed to the other parapet to see how far they went in the opposite direction. Then for the first time I noticed a house built almost at the edge of the bank which fell steeply down to the railway. Only the cutting separated it from the town, and beyond it could be seen nothing but trees lining the road, and fields on either side as far as the woods of the horizon. It was the last house of the town, and one of the newest. Not being in a street it needed not to be exactly like the rest, square, pierced with oblong windows on two sides, and blank on the other two ; but so it was, except that its lower windows looked across the railway between the thin, white posts of a verandah. A strip of garden, not more than equal to it in area, surrounded the house, and this was enclosed by rusty iron railings upon all sides. Every window was shut, and the light and air blocked out by venetian blinds painted grey. The white paint of the window frames and the verandah was dirty, but the red bricks of the walls were still harshly new and untouched by vegetation or any stain. The garden had never been cultivated : it was given over to long grasses of the unhealthy rankness peculiar to soil which is composed of builders' refuse, and the stalks were matted and beaten down so as to suggest the soaked hair of something dead. The door and gate were shut. The verandah and the white paint gave the building a pretentious air of being a pleasure house ; yet it looked over the railway at the back parts of the town, at the railway station on one hand, at the cemetery and a tall chimney on the other. It had apparently not been occupied or for a little time only, and was now empty ; or it had been used for a month at a time by perhaps half a dozen families ; certainly it had never become a house ; it was the corpse, the stillborn corpse of a house.

Beyond it, between the two lines of elms and on

either side of them, was the open country. The road was old, too, worn down like a river-bed into the sandy soil, and the elms above either side made it dark as it rose towards the north. I had not gone many yards along it when I came to a place where the bank had been excavated long ago. There was a smooth sandy floor, and behind that a firm wall of orange sand interlaced by the stony and snake-like roots of a great oak which towered up from the top of the wall; and behind the trunk the sun was a scarlet round in a dull sky at the moment of going down. It was dark and still in this hollowed place, and I had looked at it for some time before I heard the crying of a child and saw three children playing in the sand. Under the oak they had dug a cave in the sand, and a black-haired boy and a fair-haired girl were carrying away little spadefuls, while the third sat still among the roots. The two workers went silently backwards and forwards. They moved gravely and without a word, and I might have thought they were unaware of one another had they not made way for one another in their comings and goings. They worked as if in a dream and being moved by some unseen power. Their faces also were fixed and expressionless; their wide-open eyes seemed to be upon something which travelled always before them and was invisible to me. They were perhaps seven years old. The other was not more than three, and he took no notice of them as he sat, his face smeared with tears and sand, and a paper bag upon his lap. Now and then he burst out into a fresh sobbing cry just as suddenly, and not more loudly than the robin singing above his head. When he did this the little girl went up to him and shook him gently, and took a cherry from the paper bag and put it into his mouth. At this he became silent again for a little, holding the cherry-stone in one hand, and with the other rubbing his eyes. When this cure had been tried several times, and the scarlet sun had gone down out of the dull heavens, the child began to cry more steadily, and it was in vain that a cherry was put into his mouth ; for he held it a little while between his lips, and did not notice when it fell out, but sobbed on and on as if he saw nothing, heard nothing, thought nothing, felt nothing, but only sobbed.

I asked the little girl : " What is the matter with him ? "

" He wants his mother," she said.

" Where does he live ? " I asked, as I stepped towards the child, meaning to lift him up.

" Over there," she replied, pointing with her eyes to the house of the verandah.

" Then why doesn't he go home ? " I said, stopping still and thinking again chiefly of the house.

" His father is dead," said the little girl and the little boy simultaneously. Then they went on with their digging, while I turned and saw the house looking as if it had grown suddenly old in those few moments—old and haggard, and so cold that I shivered to think how cold it must be in the death-room behind the venetian blinds. The silence of the house and road was like a sea suddenly expanding infinitely about me. As I turned away, the child's sob, the song of the robin, the scream of

The Bridge at Goring.

the swifts, fell into that dark silence without breaking it, like tears into a deep sea. And I looked at the house and saw that the soul of the dead man had entered it.

Remembering this, I gave up my spiritual frivolity at Cleeve, and escaped to an inn. I suppose I had been too much taken with churchyard names in the grey evening to be quite fair to the living landlord at the inn. He was a short, heavy, fair-haired man, who had a too distinguished moustache, and talked through his nose, and had a straw hat tilted back on his neck. He and a wealthy Scotchman were talking together, and invariably—by a slight effort—agreeing with one another. His little niece came in with a flag, but he successfully put her off by saying that he had a lot of things to show her by and by, and she ran away shouting: "Uncle has a lot of things to show me." He explained to the Scotchman that he really had—"flags and things for the coronation"—"must do something"—"everybody will"—"have spent half a sovereign"—"it isn't much—but still . . ." The child, he said, was very excitable, not that there was anything wrong; oh, no; but she would make a wonderful actress. He asked the Scotchman what he would take, and then ordered two whiskies, which I understood the other to pay for. They talked of drinks and of champagne, of course. The landlord began laughing at "some *ladies*" who like it sweet. He implied huge contempt for a man who could like such stuff. Nevertheless, he hastened to say: "You don't like sweet champagne? . . . No . . . No, of course you don't. . . . Oh, yes, well, tastes differ." This naturally led to Freemasonry, and it turned out that the Scotchman had done everything as a Mason (except work in stone); had served as chairman, etc. etc., and the landlord showed great eagerness of admiration by saying: "Have you really?" several times. They returned to the subject of drink. The Scotchman announced that he took nothing but whisky, except when he had to. The landlord hastened to remark: "You are quite right. You'll live the longer for it." Then the landlord related how when he was three-quarters drunk he always found it so hard to drink champagne, which was only good, really, if you were run down, or for medicinal purposes. A very great deal of natural philosophy was uttered over those three or four glasses of whisky. After the Scotchman had gone the landlord was claimed by two young gentlemen who were staying under his roof for the fishing, boating, and alcoholic drinks. They called him "Arthur," and lured him into frivolities which he was not born to, such as arranging a band with tennis rackets, etc., for instruments, and serenading the other visitors and the inhabitants of the surrounding houses. In the intervals they fortified themselves with his whisky to such an extent that his leniency towards its effect was not to be surprised at. They also took care to keep up their reputation of commonplace luridity with the barmaid, a plain, hard-worked girl, whose smile—and, they evidently believed, everything else—was at their command. When he could slip away from these sportsmen the landlord straightened his hat and talked business to the barmaid with some anxiety and no false generosity. But they were always shouting for "Arthur" in shriller and more discordant voices until at last the second fiddle of the two burst through the door of his bedroom and rushed across and fell heavily on the other side. Then his leader went quietly to bed. The landlord turned to his accounts, and the barmaid went on washing up glasses.

CHAPTER VII

FIFTH DAY—IVINGHOE TO WATLINGTON, ON THE LOWER ICKNIELD WAY, BY ASTON CLINTON, WESTON TURVILLE, CHINNOR, AND LEWKNOR

I HAD to go back to the forking of the Icknield Way and follow the Lower road from Ivinghoe. St. Mary's Church at Ivinghoe stands pleasantly among sycamores and beeches, and next door to a small creeper-covered brewery which is next door to a decent creeper-covered house with round-topped windows and a most cool and comfortable expression. Some stout and red-faced men stood talking outside the brewery in cheerful mood. On the opposite side of the road was a green enclosed by a low railing. The village was a straggling one, and there were many newish houses, of pale brick here and there, as well as old timbered cottages. I went into a grocer's shop at the moment when they were killing a pig on the other side of the wall. Neither the shrieking nor the end of it disturbed the stout proprietor cutting up lard and the women talking of the coronation.

The road was a dull, straight one going south-westwards over the London and North Western Railway a mile north of the Upper road, and two and a half miles north-west of Tring station. It passed allotment gardens and had the company of heavy-laden telegraph-posts, whose wires cut across

Grand Junction Canal.

the terraces or " linces " of Southend Hill on the right. But if the corn-bunting sang its curst dry monotony on the telegraph-wire a blackbird also sang in an oak. Beyond the railway the road was better and had level green edges up to the roses of the high hedge on the right and the low one on the left, over which I could see across the oats to the Chilterns lying dark under the sun. On the other side of the barley, which was a cold and bluish green, rose Marsworth Church tower to the right. The reservoirs beyond the turning to Marsworth were broad and rough-edged, and with some trimmed poplars at a corner, a straight rank of trimmed elm trees near the further edge, and the line of telegraph-wires on this side, they made a foreign scene, against the background of the Chilterns, of a fascinating dreariness; one man was fishing from the bank. Crossing the canal I was in Hertfordshire, which I left at the far side of the last reservoir. These dreary waters had attracted some thickets which the sedge-warbler loved and sang in, as by the Wilstone Reservoir. The inns (where they provide for anglers) and the houses near the locks had the look of canalside and wharfside settlements, a certain squalor more than redeemed by the individuality. The unpopulated hills on the left of it, and the Vale of Aylesbury on the right, emphasized this half-urban, half-marine character. The road here was very much broken into sharp turns not always by a crossing. Immediately after the last reservoir, before the turning to Drayton Beauchamp, the road was at its best, winding between not too level green edges of unequal breadth, and hedges of thorns and roses and a few ash trees; and on the edges the grass had been cut and was lying across the low clover. Doves cooed and a lark overhead sang "as if he never would be old." Then, at a bend where a ditch came in and had a willow above it and some meadow-sweet round about, a sedge-warbler was singing, the soul of a little world ten yards across. The crossing of the road to Drayton was one I shall not forget. The sign-post pointed back to Ivinghoe, forward to Aylesbury, Buckland, and Aston Clinton, on the right to Puttenham, on the left to Drayton. There was a small crook to the left before my road went forward again. In the midst of the meeting ways the sign-post had a green triangle to stand on. Also, each road had green borders which all widened to the crossing; some of the borders had rushes. The road to Puttenham swelled up a little and fell, and over the rim showed the trees of the vale. Ahead and to the left were the wooded downs. As I left the signpost I had a very sweet, gentle-spoken "Good morning" from a traveller coming towards me, a little and rickety dark foreign man, cheerful and old, carrying a thick satchel on his back and looking neither to the right nor to the left.

Instead of going on into Akeman Street and then turning at right angles along it for a mile, I took a path half a mile on this side of it which led towards Buckland Church. Where the path crossed the first hedge, a narrow, low embankment went off to the left along the hedge, followed by the path to the church and entering at last an elmy and nettly lane. Buckland village has many elm trees, plain little houses, twisting lanes, and a "Buck's Head" in a dim corner of them. Its church is of alternating flints and freestone, but the tower all of stone. It was a very cool place with a slow, muffled, beating clock and a carpet of sun lying across the floor from the netted open door. One of the tablets on the wall was to Judith ——. High on the wall under the tower was an inscription saying :—

"Near this place, together with those of an infant daughter, lie the earthly remains of Frances Russell, relict of William Russell of Great Missenden, daughter of Edward and Frances Horwood of this place. She died October 8, 1793, aged 73 years.

"The fleeting moments of Prosperity, the tedious hours of Adversity, and the lingering illness which Providence allotted, she bore with equanimity and Christian resignation.

"Reader! Go and do likewise."

It was a rusty and dusty inscription read mostly by the bellringers standing under the tower, and one of the most dismal certificates of life, marriage, motherhood, religion, death and the philosophy of relatives that I have seen. It was cheerful afterwards to read the name of Peter Parrot on a tombstone out in the sun.

Past Buckland Church, I turned to the right and almost at once to the left along a road which went through a hayfield and then became a borderless hedged road, but with parallel marks as of traffic on the left. It came out opposite Aston Clinton Church into Akeman Street, a main road of elms, chestnuts, and telegraph-poles, going through a typical "peaceful" village street, with a smithy and a "Rose and Crown," "Swan," and "Palm in

Aston Clinton.

Hand," an advertisement of petrol, a horse's brass trappings gleaming under a tree, and in the park on the left hand a peacock proclaiming the neighbourhood of a large house. I had to turn to the right along Akeman Street for a quarter mile before turning out to the left into a road with houses facing the park. They were poor cottages, a little sordid and all jammed in a row, and three public houses amongst them. Past these houses the road was a dull, straight one under elms, with a clear view over a level beanfield to the Downs and their trees, with bright tops and dark, misty shadows below. Presently a brooklet appeared alongside the road among willow-herb and overhung by alder, elder, and willow, and at the beginning of Weston Turville it provided entertainment for half a hundred ducklings. The road went through the midst of Weston Turville and among inns on both sides and down the turnings, a " Vine," a " Chequers," a " Plough," a " Six Bells," a " Black Horse," a " Chandos," and a " Crown," followed not much beyond the church by a " Marquis of Granby " and a " Swan "—but these were at World's End. It was a village with here a house and there two or three round a square of streets, with the manor-house and elmy church tower outside it to the south; and between the houses there were intervals of garden. I noticed a little house lost between the great bare trunks of half a forest of trees in a timber merchant's yard. I found an inn which had a straight settle facing a curved one of elm with a sloping back and reasonable arm-rests. There were quoits on pegs under the ceiling, and above the usual circular target for darts ; the open fireplace had a kitchen range placed in it. The floor was composed of bluish-black and red tiles alternating.

I did not make certain how the Icknield Way went through Weston Turville, though a possible course seemed to turn left on entering the village and go by Brook Farm and Malthouse Row, and a little west of the old manor-house and by the " Vine." Unless it took some such course, it could hardly have got to Terrick and Little Kimble, but must rather have gone straight on through Stoke Mandeville, Kimblewick, and Owlswick and into the road now marked " Lower Icknield Way " at Pitch Green. I went past the Weston reservoir to World's End, and then over the Wendover and Aylesbury road only a mile north of Wendover, having clearly in view the obelisk on Coombe Hill, and a little later the towered Ellesborough Church looking ghostly in the sunlight under Beacon Hill. The hay was cut on both sides, and the road wound between broad borders of thistles and nettles. Near Terrick I saw the first meadow crane's-bill of that season and that country—the purple flower whose purple is the emblem of a rich inward burning passion. At the very edges of the roadside turf the white clover grew. In the hawthorns a blackbird sang.

Soon I came to Kimble station on the Aylesbury branch of the Great Western and Great Central Junction Railway, and some new houses, one of them named " Beware of the Dogs." Under the railway I turned left to Risborough and Longwick, not right to Hartwell. And now the road settled down to a fairly straight course for about ten miles, with meadow-sweet and rose in its low hedges and a view over the wheat to the Chilterns. It was usually about a hundred feet lower than the Upper way, and from one to two miles north of it. It was crossed by hardly any road more important than itself, except that from Thame to Princes Risborough. At this crossing, outside "The Duke of Wellington" or "Sportsman's Arms," a street organ played "Beside the Seaside" and other national anthems. Little more than a mile beyond I entered Oxfordshire. I left the road to see Chinnor Church, half a mile south, which looks southward on the juniper-dotted hills skirted by the Upper way. The most notable thing in the church was an oval tablet near the screen inscribed with the words :—

Beneath
lie
the remains of
William Turner
Esqre
who died 23rd March
1797 aged 61
"Here the wicked cease
from troubling and
the weary are
at rest."

The word "here" my fancy took quite literally, and I saw a skeleton cramped behind the tablet protesting to the living that there, inside the wall, denuded of flesh and of all organs, nerves, and desires, a wicked man ceased from troubling and a weary one could be at rest; the teeth of the skeleton shook in their dry sockets as it, now a hundred and ten years old, uttered those sweet words: "Here the wicked cease from troubling and the weary are at rest." Some of the dead outside bore formidable monosyllabic names, such as Wall, Crook, Saw, and Cocks. At the "Royal Oak" I listened for half an hour to information and complaints about the heat, which was at the time about ninety degrees in the shade, and then went out to make the most of the heat itself, which I could well do, having myself, as a good critic has pronounced, an unvarying temperature of about forty-five degrees (Fahr.).

I left the "Bird in Hand" and a squat, white windmill on the left and entered a fine green road going straight south-west. One of the hedges was high enough for shade, in the other some young chestnut trees were growing up. After some distance the left half of the road was rough and had a ditch along it; then a tiny stream flowed across, and the way lost its left hedge and went slightly raised between wheat and oats, poppy and tall, pale scabious. After that I had clover and bird's-foot trefoil and bedstraw and rest-harrow underfoot—corn on the left as far as elms in masses, and behind these the Chilterns—corn on the right and ridges of elms beyond. Then another rillet traversed the road and cooled the feet. In places the grass was very long. Crossing the road to Kingston Blount the way was more used and rougher; as before it had corn on both hands—barley and oats speckled like a partridge. Then a third rillet, and then wheat, barley, oats, and beans in turn ; on the other side of the way wych-elms. There were always elms, and here and there a farm under them, beyond the corn on the left. Aston Rowant lay near on my left, with a towered church, a big house, and men upon a rick, at the edge of the elms. To cross the Aston road my way made a slight crook to the left and then skirted the hay of Aston Rowant park, with elms and sweet limes amidst the hay: it was a good grass and clover track, not deeply rutted. Presently in the mowed and cleared fields on both sides cattle were walking out from milking. With another slight crook to the left the way crossed the High Wycombe and Stokenchurch and Oxford road, where yellow-hammers were singing in the beeches alongside the telegraph-posts. My way was now a hard road bordered by beeches and firs, through which I could see the tower of Lewknor Church across a hayfield. A willow-wren, with a voice like the sweet voice of someone a thousand years away, was singing among the tops of the trees. Below, briers and thorns were interwoven, and silver-weed grew at the edge of the dust. Some country people say that silver-weed is good for the feet, a belief which might well have no better foundation than the fact that it grows commonly close to the road which is cruel to the feet. On the right I passed a little deserted lodge with pointed windows and doorway gaping blank, and on the left a wood of beech, elm, and chestnut shadowing a wall in which there was a door barricaded almost to the lintel by nettles.

This cool wood was full of the chiding of blackbirds and one thrush's singing. Near the end this piece of road turns decidedly to the left ; but over the wall on the right are some signs of a track which had not this southward bend. At the end of the present road, but a little way to the right along the road to Wheatfield, which it enters, is Moor Court, a small old house of bricks and tiles, with wings at each side, and a massive stone chimney at the road end ; and it has a range of thatched farm buildings and a line of Lombardy poplars all enclosed in a wet moat. A little farther up, a farm road, which might have continued the track on the right of the road just quitted, turns out to the left and with a short break leads to Pyrton and Cuxham and Brightwell Baldwin and so to Wallingford ; or from Pyrton the route might be to Watcombe Manor, Britwell, and Ewelme. But the Lower Icknield Way is, to judge from the map, supposed to give up its individuality at Moor Court and make straight away through Lewknor and by Sheepcote Lane to join the Upper road. There seems no good reason why this connection between the two, if it were such, should have been more than a convenience for a few travellers, unless we suppose that the very hilly and uneven portion of the Upper road, between the beginning of the separation and Chinnor Hill, so frequently became impassable that it was abandoned for short or long periods or altogether. But as a road close to Ewelme was known in the seventeenth century as the Lower Icknield Way, I was determined to go by Ewelme. From Moor Court I went down to the pretty group of a smithy, a "Leather Bottle," and Lewknor's towered church at the crossing, where I entered the high road, making past Shirburn Castle to Watlington. At Watlington the road bends sharp to the right, and so comes into line with the Lower Icknield Way, as it was near Moor Court.

This road between the Chilterns and the corn was followed by a single line of telegraph wire. It had a slightly raised green edge on the right, marked by footpaths. It went within a few yards of the moated castle of Shirburn. Here, says the marvelling countryside, the drawbridge is nightly drawn up, presumably with the philanthropic motive of giving work to somebody. I wished to see the castle as the home of a library which has lately given to the world a collection of ballads from manuscript of the early sixteenth century—"The Shirburn Ballads." But a great length of eight-foot wall alongside the road shut off the view. It was a bad wall too, and could not be liked or admired for its own sake. I succeeded only in seeing one new battlemented tower, which, I was told, supplied water for the castle laundry. The best thing at Shirburn was almost opposite the castle entrance—a narrow strip of land raised above the road, and protected from it by a row of goodly elm trees, so that I walked between a high hedge and them in a private coolness and green gloom as of an airy church about a hundred yards long. On the hedge side of this strip there was a depression which might have been the old road: or perhaps at one time the elms stood in the middle of the road like those yonder on the Upper Icknield Way under Watlington Hill. Hereby they have set up the reputed remains of one of Queen Eleanor's funeral crosses.

Watlington.

Watlington is a big square village of no great beauty or extraordinary antiquity, all of a piece and rustic, but urban in its compression of house against house. A castle stood at the north edge near the present church. The Oxford road bounds the town on its garden side, where farm-houses begin and cottages with gardens of monkshood and roses. Near this road there was a " pleasure fair," where the roundabouts and swings of some travelling company were putting in time on their way to a bigger town and a regular engagement. There must be great wisdom in the men of Watlington, to be able to harmonize their grave, rustic streets with the town-bred music as of a steam-engine in pain. It was a feat I could not accomplish. The most I could do was to go into a taproom, where the music did not penetrate and the weary were at rest. It was a most beautiful evening, and the swifts were shrieking low down along the deserted streets at nine o'clock. I should like to see them crowded with sheep from Ilsley, and the old drover wearing a thistle in his cap, or with Welsh ponies going to Stokenchurch Fair over the Chilterns. But there is no market at Watlington, and nothing but a " pleasure " fair ; a cheap week-end railway ticket to London pleases the country people by making them feel near London, whether they go or not ; and it may encourage new residents. This was what my host wanted ; his taproom was much too peaceful for living men, though he liked well enough to smoke his last pipe there, sitting in his shirt sleeves until the silent room was quite dark and his children came home from the roundabouts. A man came heavily down the street wheeling a barrow, stopped outside and called for a pint ; while he waited he ruminated, looking down the street to the first stars and whistling " Beside the seaside, beside the sea," then he tipped up his tankard, emptied it, and went off in a determined manner.

When I went up to bed I was astonished to find a bedroom that was not at all new to me, though I had never before, to my knowledge, stopped at this inn. If it was an illusion, the pictures created it. I had certainly seen them before, in Wales, in Cornwall, in Wiltshire, and in Kent. What first caught my eye was a beauteous female of a far from slender type kneeling unharmed in the midst of roaring waters. She had on a snowy night-dress, over which her curls flowed far down in admirable disorder. The foam of the sea flew all over and round her without wetting her night-dress or taking the gloss out of her curls. Her face also seemed unaffected by her extraordinary position on a small, isolated rock in the sea, and wore an expression that would have been better suited to an afflicted lady in her own apartment. She was suffering, but not from exposure to cold and wet, and what was more extraordinary still was, that on this solitary rock she had found a quantity of thick, velvety stuff, and on this, as was natural, she was kneeling to save her tender knees from the unaccustomed rock.

On the opposite wall hung a similar picture, I suppose by the same artist, for surely there could be only one man who had these marvellous visions—visions they must have been, since no one could invent things so improbable and, without their visionary character, so ridiculous. Here also the scene was a wild sea and a rock in the midst. One beauteous girl of the same type as in the other picture was in the water, another had apparently just clambered up on to the rock. I say apparently, but her night-dress was dry, snow-white, and untorn. I say apparently, because I could only imagine that the two had been swimming together and one had got first to the rock; for it was not likely that one should find herself on a rock in this position and then by mere chance see a fellow-mortal of the same sex, age, beauty, and costume struggling with the waves close by. Her struggle was nearly over, for the beauty on the rock, kneeling on the velvet carpet which, by a fortunate accident, almost covered it, bent over in an attitude of much grace and caught her unhappy sister by one of her fair hands. The face of the swimmer was upturned and exquisitely sad, but, as in the other picture, it was not the sadness of a swimmer in stormy and dark waters, but rather of a lady inwardly tormented by some difficulty of the "heart" or of the "spirit," to use a popular physiology. Her sadness was great, and naturally so; but I should have expected to see astonishment mingled with it, because what could be seen of her night-dress was dry as it had ever been in the linen cupboard at her stately home; and her hair, though loose, was not untidy and would have pleased a lover, had she confessed one and had he, instead of another lady, been aiding her in distress. I had last seen these two pictures at Tregaron, and I sighed with a serene and pleasant recollection of the place, the season, and the company.

I was glad also to see a third work of the same artist, or at least of the same school. It belonged to a different period, geological rather than marine; and again it must be insisted that the work was visionary because no one capable of a mere invention so ridiculous is likely to have the power and the patience to execute it with such completeness and finish. The scene was midnight in a valley of rocks and of high, precipitous, rocky sides, wide enough apart to have admitted a mountain torrent of some size. But it was dry, and over the sharp rocks went a most beautiful lady. She was dressed in thin and clinging garments from her shoulders down to her ankles. To meet a woman so beautiful and so suitably and yet unusually dressed all alone in the mountains would be at least as surprising as to see her on a little rock in the sea as one was passing in a storm. I could imagine her easily upon the velvet-covered rock. Her arms were bare, and with one she clasped a book to her left breast, while with the other she felt her way along the precipitous wall of the valley and steadied herself over the cruel rocks. It was to be noticed that there was no velvet over these rocks, and this is another proof of the genuineness of the artist's vision, unless it should be suspected that he disliked the appearance of a long strip of carpet all down a valley. A fierce and extravagant vision, you will say. But the gentleness which had somehow ensured the carpet in the marine vision had not been eclipsed in the geological. From the edge of the farther wall of the valley shone a light. Someone was up there with a lantern and was turning its beams down on to the spot under the fair traveller's feet. There could be little doubt that he was following her along with the light, but he could not be seen. The lantern would have been more *natural* in a narrow alley in a town, but there was no question here of mere nature. If it comes to nature, was there ever a period when a woman of such beauty, and of very great refinement, strayed out with a book among inhospitable mountains, clad in a dress that was fitted rather to suggest and even display the form of limbs and bosom than to protect them from rocks, thorns, and weather, not to speak of men and other wild beasts ? A voluptuous Oriental or Frenchman might of course sit down and invent an earthly paradise with a small population of like beauties, but their object would be as unmistakable as it would be objectionable to persons of sensibility and discipline, except when alone or off their guard. But an Englishman or a German could only have copied such a picture from a vision having nothing to do with the flesh, and a charge of any such thing would recoil upon the accuser. I believe it was by an Englishman or a German. I should like to see some of the work of his less visionary moods. I should like to see him with his family, talking to his wife about the butcher's bill and his daughter's marriage—I should like to know if he had a daughter or a child at all. I should like to see him with his friends after dinner, and reading Mr. George Moore's *Memoirs of my Dead Life*.

I thought at one time that one of the other pictures was by the same man, partly because it is so often to be seen with his work and appeals to the same people, such as myself, and partly because it had a similar detachment from modern life; but I could not feel sure that it was the result of a vision and not of pure invention. The scene was a summer garden sloping down to a river, and at the foot of the slope a terrace of turf and a flight of steps to the water. On the terrace four girls were having tea. They were much thinner than those on the rocks; they wore white clinging dresses and their heads were bare. They were all smiling and their faces were such that no man could imagine a god, providence, fate, parent, lover, doctor or little boy in the street hard-hearted enough to interrupt the smiles. Human beings like them are not to be seen now, and no portraits or records of them in the past have come down to us. They seemed born to eat chocolate and drink sweet lemonade and never suffer from the consequences. There had been five of them, but one stood on the bottom step feeding two swans without any apparent effort. She had a hat in her hand either because a hat is more beautiful than a hand or because it is more easy to draw. She was hanging down her head thinking of something—or it might be nothing—unconnected with the swans or the slow, still river. Behind her a person whose mouth would not melt butter stood looking at her back. He was dressed in pretty breeches and buckled shoes, and was interesting chiefly as making the observer marvel what witty power had added a creature so appropriate to such a company. As marvellous must have been the artist's invention. If it could be imagined that dresses should, out of their own spirit, magically produce beings to wear them they would be like these five ladies; and if dainty breeches, silk stockings, and buckled shoes should have the same power they would unfold a man like the lover. The effect of the whole was to suggest summer, a lovely and harmless place (for the artist's fresh water would not drown, any more than his sea water would wet a night-dress), wealth, luxury, happiness, youth, frivolity, innocence, benevolence—to suggest them, especially to those who know very little of these things.

There were several pictures of scenery. One showed a steep and very romantic forest road. It was deep in snow, and enormous trees, whose roots were nourished in Hades, towered up above on either hand, but let in the light of a full moon that shone straight down the road. Towards the moon and up the road went a tall, mantled traveller, leaning on a staff and turning his head to look into the wood. The picture had no name, text, or explanation. It was a nameless man and a nameless traveller, both unknown to history. Nothing was happening. It was simply a combination of four or five grand, simple elements; a mighty forest—a moon—snow—a solitary road—a tall traveller.

One of the other pictures was the same, except that a foaming river took the place of the snowy road. The forest and the moon were the same. The traveller was not there, and to one who had seen the last picture there was a touch of tragedy in his absence which atoned for it; he might have been surprised at the very moment when the snowy road was being changed into a foaming river. Those who had not seen the other had to be content with a moon, a romantic forest, a river running down through it, and foam instead of snow. It hardly seemed to me to be enough—lacking the human interest. A small flock of sheep among the trees, with or even without a shepherd, would have made a vital difference, and the picture could then also have been recognized by purchasers and recipients of Christmas cards. And this picture was one which would appeal to those who knew the kind of thing depicted. Rough woodlanders and their wives, people who have suffered in snow, poor men who have travelled alone and leaned on their staffs, would gladly put both pictures on their walls. There were photographs of such people on the mantelpiece, people whom no best clothes or photographer's polish could turn into poetic heroes or cigar-box beauties; men with queer hairy faces, legs bent like oak branches, and eyes squinting at the photographer; women their equals, but if anything more hardened, more tortured, more smiling upon the occasion of being photographed.

Between photographs of a gamekeeper, whose face was like a furze bush with eyes in it, and a card of mourning for Jane Mary Sims, aged seventy-three, hung a picture seeming to have little to do with either. It was of a high-born and well-dressed lady with regular features and graceful, mature figure sitting beside a cradled child. She was bending over towards the child, and her face, though composed, was sorrowful. Had she looked up she would have seen an unusual sight, and it was a mercy that she did not, for it would have certainly upset her composure through astonishment and fear. For not many feet from her was the head of a human being who was coming towards her head foremost through the window, or more probably the ceiling. I say a human being because her body —it was a mature and athletic, slender lady—was of the same general form, size, and proportions as those of our own species, and she wore the clinging night-dress so much favoured by the visionary artist. But she had wings attached to her shoulders, not large enough to be of any use, supposing her to have learned their management, but sufficient to make part of a becoming fancy dress or fairy dancing costume. She had apparently dived from some height, and in a bewitching attitude was making straight for the cradle. As she was no Ariel's sister capable of playing "i' th' plighted clouds," the danger both to her and to the cradle was great. She faced it with no sign of fear, her soft eyes and her even and not too full lips expressing a mind in tranquillity and scarcely, if at all, stirred by expectation or surmise. There was no sequel to this daring but painful picture, nor, of course, any explanation. It was, I should say, the fancy of a genius who had mingled the common and the improbable in dreams produced by opium or other drug.

CHAPTER VIII

SIXTH DAY—WATLINGTON TO UPTON, BY EWELME, WALLINGFORD, LITTLE STOKE, THE PAPIST WAY, LOLLINGDON, ASTON, AND BLEWBURY

FOR supper, bed, and picture gallery my host at Watlington charged me two shillings, and called me at five into the bargain, as I wished to breakfast at Wallingford. I took the turning to Ewelme out of the Oxford road, and was soon high up among large, low-hedged fields of undulating arable, with here and there a mass or a troop of elms at a corner, above a farm, or down a hedge. Farther away on the left I had the Chilterns, wooded on their crests and in their hollows, not very high, but shapely. The sky was misted at the horizon, but overhead milky blue, with thin-spun, dim white cloud; the sun a burning disc; half-way up the sky hung heavier white clouds, which might develop later. The road was clover-edged, winding, and undulating, and by no means an improbable connection of the Icknield Way. Britwell Salome Church lay on my right, across a willowy field, and having no tower or spire, it was like one of the farm buildings surrounding it. Then my road mounted between nettly and elmy banks, and had a bit of waste on the right where chalk had been dug—a pretty tumbled piece, all nettles and gix and white bryony under ash trees. There was not much hedge between the road and the corn before I got to the "Plough" at

Watlington Town Hall.

Britwell Salome, and next the "Sun." The village was scattered among trees, not interrupting the smell of hay. The road skirted it, and was soon out again amongst the wheat, and passing Britwell park, where the cattle were crossing in a straight line between groups of elms. In the hedge there was bracken along with the yellow bedstraw and white bryony. For a time there were gorse and bracken together on the green strip above the road. Then, instead of going straight on to Benson, I turned to the left for Firebrass Hill, Ewelme, and Wallingford. Beyond this turn all the country round was high, bare cornland undulating to the darker hills. The road had nettles for a hedge, or sometimes brier, scabious, knap-weed, and rest-harrow, and once some more purple meadow crane's-bill; it had steep banks, but no green border. But this was not the Icknield Way, which would never have dipped down to the lower part of Ewelme and up again at once. The first houses of the village were decent, small ones, standing high and looking down at the farm-house thatch, the cottages, gardens of fruit trees, and elms of the main village. The churchyard covered the slope down from the upper to the lower village, and in the midst stood the church, a venerable one with a particularly neat growth of ivy across the tower. I could not get into the church, but could hear the clock ticking in the emptiness. In the churchyard I noticed this devout fancy over the body of Alice Heath, who died in 1776 :—

Kind angels, watch this sleeping dust
Till Jesus comes to raise the just ;
Then may they wake with sweet surprise
And in their Saviour's image rise.

I should like to know what was in the verse-writer's mind when he penned the first line. The word "surprise" pleased me most, though due to a rhyme. It occurred to me that the writer's mind, through grief, might have been in the same condition as the bedroom artist at Watlington who drew the lady and the cradle and the beautiful winged diver. I believe that this artist would have translated literally into pictorial form the words :—

Kind angels, watch this sleeping dust.

He would have shown a neat, grassy churchyard with an immemorial church tower in the background. Scattered over the turf close to the church would be an indistinct crowd of tombstones. Nearer and clearer he would present a new and costly stone, probably in the form of a cross, standing at the top of three or four steps. Many wreaths of rare and costly flowers would lie unfaded at the foot of the steps. On the lowest step two figures of exceptional beauty and dignity would be kneeling without sign of impatience or any other emotion. They would be in the customary costume of these pictures, and the onlooker would marvel what they were doing ; and if he knew that they were watching the dust below, he would still conjecture as to what they were to watch against, and how they proposed to resist the attempts of any robbing man, beast, dragon, or other monster. But it is unlikely that any such picture was in the mind of the Ewelme epitaph-writer. He or she had perhaps no distinct image ; choosing words that would fit the metre and not be in any way surprising to the religious, he thought of "angels" and of "dust," and the need of epithets pretty soon suggested "kind" and "sleeping." Nevertheless, when I read it I came so near to forming an image, rather in the style of the bedroom artist, that it is possible the writer had an image or vision of some sort, and handed it on to me in that early July morning before anyone was on the roads or in the churchyard.

There was a much better stone and delicately writ inscription near the east window. The stone, a very thin, shouldered one, had slipped down into the earth, and was less than two feet in height and in breadth. The words were :—

> Here lyeth the Body
> of Margaret Machen
> who departed this
> life the 5th of April
> being aged 20 years
> Anno Dom. 1675.

Here the smallness and prettiness of the thin stone, its being half swallowed up in earth and grass, the fineness of the written, not printed, lettering, the name a poem in itself and half Welsh, the youth of the girl, her death in April more than two hundred years ago, all together produced an effect like that of beauty, nay! which was beauty. Not far off was a ponderous square chest with as much reading on it as a page of newspaper, dated 1869. The sparrows were chittering in the elms.

My road dipped down through the village, and to the left by the "Greyhound" and up between steep banks under larch trees. On the right a few yards up that road a footpath used to go for two miles towards Wallingford, but it was covered by corn for the first part, and I kept to the road. I was soon going past the Ewelme cow common again, but along the opposite side; and there were cows among its thorns. For a few yards, after crossing the Benson and Dorchester road at Gypsies'

Ewelme Cow Common.

Corner, I was in the Upper Icknield Way again, but turned to the right, due west, leaving Clack's Farm on the south instead of the west. I was then going down towards the green-striped cornland, the clustered trees of the Thames Valley, and the pale spire and tower of Wallingford rising out of it. The low, long curves of land meeting or intersecting a little above the river were like those of a brier with nothing to climb. In the hedges there were wild roses and masses of traveller's joy, with all its grey-green buds very large. Instead of following the road round its bend to the south-west, I turned just past the bend into a green lane to the right, which made straight for Walling-

Wallingford Bridge.

ford spire; and into this lane presently came the foot-path from Ewelme and a parallel old lane. However, I had to turn sharp to the left to reach Crowmarsh Gifford and Wallingford. Crowmarsh is a wide street of old cottages leading to Wallingford bridge. Wallingford climbs the right bank up from the bridge, and out of its crowded brick rise the tower and the spire of two churches, and the ivied tower of a castle, of the kind that looks as if it had been ready-made ruinous and ivied, with a flag-staff on top. I crossed the bridge to the town, and went up the narrow, old street, past an inn called "The Shakespeare," to the small square of small shops, where red and blue implements of farming stood by the pillared town hall and the sun poured on them. I went into the "private bar" of an inn, but hearing only a blue-bottle and seeing little but a polished table, and smelling nothing else, I went out and round the corner to the taproom of the same inn. Here there were men, politics, crops, beer, and shag tobacco.

This contrast between the "private bar" and the taproom round the corner reminded me of another town which illustrates it perfectly. At the edge of the town, its large front windows looking up the principal street, its small back windows over a windy common to noble hills, is a public house called "The Jolly Drover." The tap of "The Jolly Drover" is the one blot upon the face of Coldiston. The town is clean and demure from the decent old houses of the market-place to the brand-new cottages, more like conservatories than dwellings, on the outskirts. The magistrates are busy week after week in sentencing men and women of all ages for begging, asking for hot water to make tea, sleeping under hedges or in barns, for being unseemly in act or speech ; if possible, nothing offensive must happen in the streets. A market is held once a week and is a byword in the county. Any animal can be offered for sale there; the drover creeps along behind a beast that attracts as much attention as a menagerie in the wayside villages; they know where it is going ; they have seen a pig resembling a greyhound, except that it had not the strength to stand up, sold there for a shilling. Three or four times a year a builder and contractor of Coldiston is sold up, because he has been trying to get work by doing it for nothing, and these sales are the chief diversion of the neighbourhood. The town is a model of neatness and respectability, as if created by a shop-window decorator ; and of all the public-houses—all named hotels—" The Jolly Drover " is the neatest and most respectable outside, and the most expensive inside. It is painted white at short intervals. The chief barmaid is a Londoner, white-faced and coral-lipped, with a love-lock over her marble brow; and her way is brisk and knowing, and her speech more than equal to the demands made upon it of an evening by the tradesmen who will come until they are rich enough to quit the town for ever. Every form of invitation adorns the exterior.

But round the corner, towards the common, " The Jolly Drover " is white no longer. It has no pavement outside, but a space of bare earth overshadowed by an enormous elm's last two living branches and roughened by its wide-spreading roots. There is no invitation to enter here, but simply the words upon a low lamp, " The Jolly Drover Tap." No invitation is needed, for the windows are not curtained and the passer-by cannot fail to see the contented backs of drinkers and the long tiers of bottles. At night almost as much can be seen through the yellow blinds. The door stands open opposite the old tree, and through it the eye finds the bar, the plain country barmaid, the lamp, and the bright bottles. A mongrel dog or two and a gypsy's broken-down cart and wild-eyed horse are usually outside, or a tramp's woman waiting, or a group of men talking quietly before going in or after coming out. Here "The Jolly Drover" answers to its name. It is a hedge public house of old red brick and tiles, joined, nevertheless, to the white-fronted hotel and connected with it in the proprietor's accounts. It is noisy. They sing there. No plain man is afraid to go in who has the price of half a pint in his pocket. In the summer benches are set outside, and men can sit and see the discreet going to and fro of the town life a few yards away.

Old Jack Runaway (who will borrow sixpence and then lose half a year's custom in watercress for fear of showing his face again) has lost six heifers that he was taking to the fair over the hill, but he has a pint inside and a pint before him—the clock stands still—and as the people go by he comments to himself :—

"My young Lord Drapery, may he go to gaol for being a poor beggar before he's forty. A brood mare; what with living between a policeman and a postman, with a registrar in front and a minister behind, *her* children ought to be tin soldiers. Now

I wonder what's *he* worth? But if I was coined into golden sovereigns I wouldn't have married his missus when I was twenty, no, I wouldn't. Pretty Miss Ladybird, Ladybird, Ladybird, fly away from home; you're a tantalizer for a fine day, to be out with a young chap drinking a glass of six and nobody looking. What we do lose by being old, to be sure, more than by being poor! What a clean, white beard, now, that Mr. Welcome has got, like an angel. Eh, old Colonel High and Mighty, there's doctors for sciatica and gout, but there's something we have both got by being sixty that they won't cure, not if your purse is as long as your two legs. How much do *you* weigh, bombarrel? They don't allow a carriage and pair in Kingdom Come. Now, *that* young fellow could break a good few stones on a summer's day; kind, too, and don't his heels kick the pavement proud; but mind the women don't bend your back for you, or you might as well be dust to dust any day. That's what I call a good piece, neat and not too stuck up, not so young as she was, keeps the house tidy, and knows where they sell the best things cheap; now, I'd like to walk into your parlour and have a cup of tea, missus, after wiping my feet on the mat and hanging up my hat; and then that little ladybird of a nursemaid brings in the baby, and we feed it on cake and weak tea; it must be weak, or it's bad for the health . . .; and wouldn't I be proud to have you brushing my coat as I goes out of a morning, a black coat, and putting a rose in my button-hole, and kissing me before all the street—ha, ha! dirty Jack Runaway. How they do dress up the youngsters these days, like little angels; hark at them talking, and when the mother whispers to them and they run over as if you dropped it and give you a penny, you might think it would turn into a flower in their hands, and they give you a kind of look as much as to say, 'God is feeding His sparrows,' and then they run away without a word, and you look at the price of half a pint, and either you bless them or else you curse them. *You*, Reverend Sir, would give me a cold in the head if you were to talk; then you'd give me sixpence; if you go to heaven, there's a bit of luck left for those who don't, you freezing point, you Monday's loaf, you black-and-white undertaker's friend. Oh, this town! it's rotten without stinking, gilt without gingerbread. Look at them staring at us as if we were wild beasts taking an airing *outside* the cage. . . ."

The town in its turn does watch "The Jolly Drover Tap" and its life. Why should there be all that space wasted where the elm stands? people wonder; it is quite old-fashioned, and they smile pityingly, yet tenderly, when the old tree is crowding into leaf. But when there are half a dozen rough men and women talking aloud and gesticulating like foreigners over the price of a long, brown dog that shivers under a cart, they do not see why it should be so; only, it is "The Jolly Drover," and rather difficult to attack. It is extraordinary, they think as they pass by the turning down to the Tap, how a lot of lazy fellows, with nothing to do and with only rags on them, can get enough to spend half a day there. That ought certainly not to be allowed. These are not the honest poor. Either a man must work, or be looking out for work in a serious manner, or be so well dressed that he obviously need not work ; or something is wrong. Nor do they invariably look starved and miserable. They eat and drink and talk to one another. Where do they come from ? Of course they do not live in Coldiston: then why come here to drink ? They cannot, of course, be stuffed into prison or workhouse or asylum ; but is there no other cesspool possible in an age with a genius for sanitation ?

When the blinds are down and the lamp lit, what a jolly place it is ! The light pours out through the door on to the old tree, and makes it look friendly as you go in, and romantic as you come out. It is best at haymaking or harvest time in fine weather. The irregular labourers come into the town, especially on a Saturday, and break their journey at "The Jolly Drover Tap." The townsman glances in as he passes, and sees a tall, straight man in a restful attitude standing up at the bar, and he has just raised his pot to drink. It is only a glimpse of a second, but it remains in the mind. The passer-by could not say how the drinker was clad, except that he wore a loose, broad-brimmed hat on his head, pushed back so as to leave quite clear against the lamp the whole of a big-featured, long face, the brow, and the curled hair up to the crown. Was it coat and trousers, or just shirt and trousers ? At any rate the whole man could be seen underneath. Not that the observer did not as a rule admire a man fully and fashionably dressed. Only, in this light, just this harvest evening of purple and of great silence, the tall man drinking with head thrown back at the end of the passage looked more like the statues of a bygone age, or the representations of magnificent men seen in pictures, or the soldiers he has read of in books about the wars of Roundhead and Cavalier or the invasions of Wales and Scotland—yes! the height and carriage of this man call up the words "rough borderer." A lance or a long sword would look well in his hands. His hat is not unlike a foot-soldier's helmet. And then the face—coarse, fearless, and careless—is an enigma. He is some fellow without a house, or wife, or any goods or gods, yet this is how the admirer used to picture lords and generals when a little boy at school. He is not thinking about rent, accounts, education, clothes, the poor, church, chapel, appendicitis, or this time next year. He is not apparently in a hurry. He has no vote, and one party in power is as good as the other to him. No doubt a wasteful fellow—has fallen, perhaps, through drink—is good-natured possibly, but would not stop short at violence on occasion—idle with all his strength—and yet . . . And yet? The figure and face against the light stick in the mind of the man out in the street. He is discontented. He grumbles at his wife when he goes in because she has not done something, and he does more, he grows enraged, when he finds that she really has done it, but has not had time to tell him. He lies still in bed on his back, thinking for a long time. His wife lies still, and he knows that she also is awake thinking. He says " Good night," hoping she will say something to comfort him for his fruitless wakefulness. But she says " Good night," and no more. They remain silent. He has the image of the drinker clear in the darkness before he falls asleep. Left entirely alone his wife sighs, and presently she also is asleep.

But I do not wish to say that Wallingford is as respectable as Coldiston. All I can say is that the ford below is very old, and it is highly probable that some travellers on the Icknield Way followed the road I had been on from Gypsies' Corner to Wallingford and then into the Berkshire Ickleton Street at Blewbury, if not before. Others, avoiding Wallingford, might have crossed at Little Stoke, from which a westward road goes up, called the " Papist Way."

From Wallingford I made for the " Papist Way," following a series of paths and roads about a quarter of a mile east of the river. I went past the little towerless and spireless church of Newnham Murren, which had a number of crooked, ivy-coloured tombstones, and was itself covered with ivy, which traveller's joy was beginning to climb. Then over Grim's Ditch, a mile and a half west of the Icknield Way crossing, I came to Mongewell park, and my path was along a line of huge elms and sweet limes. On my left, the main road and its telegraph wires ran bordered with charlock along the top of a low ridge above these meadows. From North

Stoke there was a good road. I turned aside to the church, but found what was better, a big range of tiled, thatched sheds and barns extending on either side of my path, with a cattle-yard in the midst full of dazzling straw and richly-stinking cow dung, and a big black sow lying on it like a recumbent statue on a huge pedestal. Swifts were shrieking above and chickens clucking in the corners. From the road the tiled church and the thatched barn fell into line, and seemed one, especially as the farm pigeons were perched on the ridges of both. On a corn-rick behind I saw the figure of a sheep on a weather-vane. This road went alongside hedgeless barley on the left, over which I could see the bare, low hills between me and the Icknield Way, and far beyond them the wooded hills about Nuffield and Nettlebed; on the right there was hay to the river; there was succory on the roadside, scabious, knapweed, rest-harrow, and long grass.

To reach the ferry at Little Stoke I turned off to the right under elm trees and was rowed across. The boy told me that the road up from the ferry was called Asylum Road, there being a big, red lunatic asylum on the right-hand side of it, just as it crossed the Reading and Wallingford road. Only beyond this crossing is it marked "Papist Way" on the map. I have not discovered why it was named so, for the name suggests too late a date to be connected with the monastery which lay near where the road reaches the Great Western railway station at Cholsey. It points to the Astons, Blewbury, and Upton, and may at one time have formed part of a road running through them to Wantage; unless this road is rather a protraction of the road from South Stoke and Moulsford, which may, however, have joined the "Papist Way" at Lollingdon.

They were talking about roads at the "Morning Star" on the left side of the "Papist Way." The fat drayman and the smart butcher's boy agreed that motor-cars were ruining the good roads. The rubber wheels can travel on the smoothest possible surface, which is the modern ideal. Hoofs, on the other hand, need something to bite into. The drayman, with his heavy waggon, would do away with steam-rollers. Here the needy cyclist interrupted, and said that he had never known better times; the smooth roads were as good for him as for motor-cars. All cursed their dust, their stink, their insolence, and all looked with some admiration at the foreign-looking chauffeur who came in for a glass and out again in a minute. Outside, the flies were "terrifying" the horses for the first time in the summer, and the drivers inside yelled at them, but seldom moved from their beer. One driver was a man with big, red ears, and a serious, quizzical face, with a beard. He came in wearing a fine musk thistle, which he seemed to think was Scotch, but immediately on being given a bunch of sweet peas he threw it away. If this had been his preference it would have been absurd enough—as if a musk thistle were not better than all the sweet peas ever contrived by man and God!—but he took the garden flowers because they were things having a price, and because they were a gift.

The "Papist Way" was a hard road winding between wheat and beans for half a mile. Then it crossed the Wallingford and Cholsey road, and

By Lollingdon Farm.

was interrupted by the railway embankment. Its course on the farther side of this seemed to be marked by a division between barley and potatoes to the left of the present road. This line was continued through Pancroft farm-yard, from which a path went south-westward along the hedges to Lollingdon. This was over black, rushy lands haunted by pewits. The road a little on the left, leading also to Lollingdon Farm, was on better ground, winding westward under the wooded swell of the round hill called Lollingdon Hill. The farm had a big home meadow with ash and poplar enclosing it, almost as if it had been a quadrangle with cloisters round. There were many thatched farm buildings in the corner, and a fine walnut tree and a beautiful abundance of poppies and dusty nettle and dusty mallow against the walls. The road had an elmy hedge on its right, but nothing on the left between it and the oats that reached up to the beeches of Lollingdon Hill-top. The long grass and knapweed and succory by the roadside were blossoming with white and meadow-brown butterflies, which flew away from their stalks as ducklings swim away from their unamphibious foster-mothers. The butterflies flew after one another, sometimes a white after a brown. The sun was perfect for them, there being fewer clouds than there were eight hours back—for as I walked I heard a pleasant, gong-like bell strike two at Aston.

Aston Tirrold and Aston Upthorpe make a square of roads with many lanes and paths crossing from one side to another. In the square are big houses and small, and their gardens and old, nettly orchards, and many sycamores, elms, chestnuts, and acacias in the gardens and along the paths; there are even some small fields within it.

Running water goes through it. Here you pass a mud wall, there a hedge, here a boarded, there a thatched, and again a tiled, cottage. At some of the corners and in the churchyard stand lime trees. If a happy child had all the ingredients of old villages to play with, it would, if it were ingenious, probably combine them thus. The farms are all outside the square but close to it. The churches are near the edge but within it. I hardly believed that anybody remained alive in the village until I failed to open the door of Aston Tirrold Church. Aston Upthorpe church was a small tiled building with a stupid little spire stuck on yesterday, to show that it was not part of the neighbouring tiled farm and outhouses. The village hid itself well on both sides under its elms. From the east it seemed all trees and orchards, from the west only the new thatch of a rick betrayed it.

My road led along the south side of the village and commanded a simple, perfect piece of downland—a bare, even wall of down with an almost straight ridge, which was also bare but for one clump; along the foot of the wall ran the main road to Wantage; up from it, an old trackway, very deeply worn, rose slanting and showing one old steep green bank, up to the ridge and over; and at the point where the trackway crossed the main road the turf was carved by a chalk-pit.

A broad track and several parallel paths went fairly straight without hedges, westward through the corn to Blewbury, passing close under the south side of a bare, sudden hill—Blewburton Hill—and the ramparts of a supposed Danish camp. Blewbury was like Aston, with a streamlet, many trees and

Blewbury.

orchards, and a towered church standing in the midst of several paths and roads. The clock was beating slowly with such gigantic and ancient peace inside the church that I did not enter. It was as if some hoary giant were sleeping inside away from the sun, if indeed he had not been there for some centuries. Outside the church lay a dilapidated and weed-grown pair of prostrate effigies. If it were not disturbing the sleeper in Blewbury Church I should suggest that these effigies might be taken in. They are much to be preferred to the clean effigies which have never borne the weather of God or the pocket-knives of men; but if they are left outside much longer they will hardly pass as representations of two human beings lying on their backs.

The south side of Blewbury touched the main Reading and Wantage road, and had several inns: a "Barley Mow," a "Catherine Wheel," a "George and Dragon," a "Sawyer's Arms," a "Load of Mischief," and at its west end a "New Inn." I was glad to see that the "Load of Mischief" still upheld its sign and name. I feared that it might have been renamed "The Red Lion" or the "Crown," and have been robbed of its sign. But there was the sign, and almost opposite a window, where I was equally glad and surprised to see an advertisement of "Votes for Women." The "Load of Mischief" was a woman, of a type belonging to a day hardly later than Hogarth's, mounted on the shoulders of a man. The man was a mere small beast of burden. The woman was magnificent—a huge, lusty, brown virago—and she was holding in her hand a glass clearly labelled "GIN." This woman and her ill-chosen spouse were painted on both sides of the sign-board, so that all coming from north and from south should see it. I forgot to inquire whether "The Load of Mischief" was a fully licensed house and sold gin. Probably it was. The sign was not a beerhouse's defamation of gin. It did not deny that gin was a very good thing. It did not assert anything more than that a big, gin-drinking woman on a small man's shoulders was a "load of mischief." How impossible it is—even in this sporting country—to think of a sign depicting a big, gin-drinking man on a little woman's shoulders. No woman ever painted a sign-board, I suppose, and no woman keeping an inn would put up such a one as "The Load of Mischief." A woman who drank gin was a load of mischief. On the other hand, a man who made the gin for her, provided that he grew rich on it, became a justice of the peace or a member of Parliament; if his father made it he became a bishop. It is the difference between mind and matter, between brain-work and manual labour. The member of Parliament or the bishop's father had only to think about gin; he might never have tasted it. The woman had to swallow it and pay for it. Therefore she grew poor while he grew rich. A history of England was once written entirely to show this difference, to insist upon it, and to teach the consumer that he must never forget his duties and responsibilities to the manufacturer, and to remind the manufacturer of his privileges. It was called "A History of England for Shoe-Blacks and Sons of Gentlemen: or, A Guide to Tuft-hunting, Sycophancy, Boot-licking, and other Services to the

Aristocracy and Plutocracy, and to Keeping in Your Place." It was published in 1911, and is used in schools.

When I went into one of the inns there was a woman seated in the taproom drinking beer, a shrill and lean, large-eyed woman of middle age, somewhat in liquor, and with ill-fitting boots, in which she had walked fifteen miles and had nine still to do. Whether or not because he had drunk more, her husband had gone on by train; she said she had "sent him." She foresaw that it was not going to rain that day. She claimed no credit for the foresight. Her corns alone had the power. In about a quarter of an hour she left. She was a woman that walked fast but stopped often. She carried her hands in the pockets of her black skirt. Not long after she had started the rain fell down upon her, as it did upon the roofs, mackintoshes, and umbrellas of the brewers, publicans, and brewery shareholders.

From the west of Blewbury to Upton there was another mile of broad, green tracks through corn, without a tree between them and the round, smooth downs, with their tumuli clear against the sky on the left hand. At Upton this series of roads from Little Stoke entered the main road, or crossed it, and continued without touching any villages on the way to Lockinge and Wantage. But this further road was a continuation of the line of the main road before it turned north to Upton and west to Hagbourne, and might have been an alternative course to Wantage, or part of an earlier way, perhaps the Icknield Way itself, which some have supposed to go nearer the Downs than the main road now does. As I meant at another time to travel this road and its parallels from Streatley to the Wiltshire border, I returned to Blewbury, and at one of the six inns read James Montgomery's *Pelican Island,* a poem of A.D. 1827, in nine cantos. The poem seemed to have been started and carried on under the influence of an ecstasy given to the author by an explorer's book. In his *Voyage to Terra Australis,* then not long published, Captain Matthew Flinders had described two little islands, the breeding-place and antique cemetery of pelicans, "islets of a hidden lagoon of an uninhabited island, situate upon an unknown coast, near the antipodes of Europe." This evidently impressed Montgomery with a strong feeling of solitariness. He imagined himself alone when "sky, sun, and sea were all the universe," himself a spirit, "all eye, ear, thought"—"what the soul can make itself at pleasure, that I was." For "thrice a thousand years" he saw none but the people of the sea :—

> Beings for whom the universe was made,
> Yet none of kindred with myself. In vain
> I strove to waken sympathy in breasts
> Cold as the element in which they moved,
> And inaccessible to fellowship
> With me, as sun and stars, as winds and vapours.

Under the sea also he saw :—

> Relics huge and strange
> Of the old world that perish'd by the flood,
> Kept under chains of darkness till the judgment.

He watched the making of a coral islet, compared with which men's work seemed nothing. A comparison which set him thinking of the grandeurs of earth, among them of Babylon, built for eternity, though where it stood,

> Ruin itself stands still for lack of work,
> And Desolation keeps unbroken Sabbath. . . .

He saw the islet grow and become hospitable. The sea-wrack and many sea-changed things were swept up on to it,

> While heaven's dew
> Fell on the sterile wilderness as sweetly
> As though it were the garden of the Lord.

Grass grew. Insects swarmed. He witnessed "the age of gold in that green isle." Trees and flowers rose up. Reptiles and amphibious monsters appeared. Then came "more admirable" beings:—

> Flocking from every point of heaven, and filling
> Eye, ear, and mind with objects, sounds, emotions
> Akin to livelier sympathy and love
> Than reptiles, fishes, insects could inspire;
> —Birds, the free tenants of land, air, and ocean,
> Their forms all symmetry, their motions grace;
> In plumage, delicate and beautiful,
> Thick without burthen, close as fishes' scales,
> Or loose as full-blown poppies to the breeze;
> With wings that might have had a soul within them,
> They bore their owners by such sweet enchantment;
> Birds, small and great, of endless shapes and colours,
> Here flew and perched, there swam and dived at pleasure;
> Watchful and agile, uttering voices wild
> And harsh, yet in accordance with the waves
> Upon the beach, the winds in caverns moaning,
> Or winds and waves abroad upon the water.

His was an eager, rapturous temperament. Next to birds he seems to have loved the insect legions—" children of light and air and fire " he calls them,

> Their lives all ecstasy and quick cross motion.

But birds and insects did not confine his sympathy. They did not, e.g., turn it aside from the elephant, leading his quiet life " among his old contemporary trees."

Whether it was through the impulse of the discoverer's words, or, as is more likely, through his own nature, he was able to suggest with some power the world that does without men, the " sterile wilderness " not neglected by the dew, the Paradise without man and without death, where

> Bliss had newly
> Alighted, and shut close his rainbow wings,
> To rest at ease, nor dread intruding ill.

I think he was enchanted by those tropical

> Airy aisles and living colonnades,
> Where nations might have worshipp'd God in peace.

For, with an energy which a tree would call religious, he describes their flourishing, and how the Indian fig was multiplied :—

> From year to year their fruits ungather'd fall ;
> Not lost, but quickening where they lay, they struck
> Root downward, and brake forth on every hand,
> Till the strong saplings, rank and file, stood up,
> A mighty army, which o'erran the isle,
> And changed the wilderness into a forest.

His love of things that are not men, that are happy and without conscience, is more instinctive than his desire for men in his solitude. They, though " kindred spirits," never moved him to a picture like the flamingoes flying,

Till, on some lonely coast alighting,
Again their gorgeous cohort took the field.

I was not surprised, then, at the seventh canto, to find him saying, in Wordsworthian strain, that we only begin to live

From that fine point,
Which memory dwells on, with the morning star,
The earliest note we heard the cuckoo sing,
Or the first daisy that we ever pluck'd,
When thoughts themselves were stars, and birds, and flowers,
Pure brilliance, simplest music, wild perfume.

My copy of the book was printed in 1827. It had the date 1856 under the old owner's name; and I suppose that not many editions have been published since 1827, or any since 1856. Yet this individual character of the writer, original as much in degree as in kind, had kept the book alive. The energy of his ecstasy gave his blank verse a gushing flow that may cause sleep, but seldom impatience, and never contempt. The overflowing of so many lines into an extra unaccented syllable seemed a natural effect of his possession by his subject, and not a device or a mere habit. At its best it had the eloquence of an improvisation.

As I shut this book it reminded me of a poem called *To Deck a Woman*, by Mr. Ralph Hodgson, where a similar rapt picture of a manless Eden is painted, but with a passion that is controlled to a quivering repose by an art finer than Montgomery's. There the passion is double, for the poet's love of the life and beauty of birds is turned to an anger too deep for hate against the woman Bloodwant, "shrill for Beauty's veins," and the men who satisfy—and provoke—her desire for feathers. The same poet's *Stupidity Street* is a curious instance of passion submitting itself to the quietest of smiling rhymes :—

I saw with open eyes
Singing birds sweet
Sold in the shops for
The people to eat,
Sold in the shops of
Stupidity Street.

I saw in vision
The worm in the wheat
And in the shops nothing
For people to eat,
Nothing for sale in
Stupidity Street.

I was glad that I had taken *Pelican Island* with me as my only book ; for if I had not I might very likely never have read it. Yet it might have escaped me even though it was in my pocket. Unless a man always carries a book with him, when he does take one it is often a little too well chosen, or rather chosen too deliberately, because it is a very good one, or is just the right one, or is one that ought to be read. But walking is apt to relieve him of the kind of conscience that obeys such choices. At best he opens the book and yawns and shuts it. He may look about him for any distraction rather than this book. He reads through a country newspaper, beginning and ending with the advertisements. He looks at every picture in an illustrated magazine. He looks out of the window for some temptation. He takes down *The Lamplighter* or Mrs. Humphry Ward's *East Lynne* from the landlord's shelves. He looks through the magazine again. If he opens the choice book he finds in it an irresistible command to go to bed at nine o'clock. The same book may be taken out thus a score of times, and acquire a friendly and well-read appearance.

CHAPTER IX

SEVENTH DAY—STREATLEY TO SPARSHOLT, ON THE RIDGEWAY, BY SCUTCHAMER KNOB AND LETCOMBE CASTLE

WHEN I was next at Streatley I took the Ridgeway westward chiefly because I like the Ridgeway, partly because I wished to see it again, now that it had to give up the title conferred on it by Bishop Bennet, of the Icknield Way. I went up from the bridge and at the "Bull" turned to the right and northward along the Wantage road, which is probably the Icknield Way. After getting well up on the chalk above the river this road maintains the same level of from two to three hundred feet, and for two miles keeps within a mile of the river on a terrace half-way up the slope of the hills. Streatley had spread itself in red spots along the side of the road, past the fork to Wallingford and up to where the Ridgeway turns off to the left and westward into the long coombe leading to Streatley Warren. At its mouth this coombe was wide and shallow, and was all grass, except on the left hand where there were new houses. In places, as by Rectory Farm, the road, a hard one, had a pleasant green terrace above it with wild roses rambling over it.

The coombe deepened and the road ascended above a golf course near Warren Farm. Thus far it was hedged, but soon, still mounting the right wall of the long coombe, it was rough and hedgeless, and old parallel tracks were to be seen above and below it. It was now near the southern edge of Thurle Down Woods on its right. Below, on the left, were the steep walls of the winding coombe,

Ridgeway, near Streatley.

dotted by thorn, juniper, and elder, and here called Streatley Warren. Of the unwooded coombes or inlets into the downs this is one of the most pleasing to me, and I shall always remember it, as I do the great coombe winding into Butser Hill on the north side, and others of those vast turf halls which the sky roofs. As it passed the head of the coombe the road was six hundred feet up, going a little north of westwards between sheep on the left and corn on the right. It was two or three miles or more from the villages on the north, Moulsford, Cholsey, the Astons, and Blewbury, and two or three hundred feet above them ; it was almost as far away from the Wantage road, and as far above it. The villages on the south were nearer, but not within a mile—Aldworth, the Comptons, and East Ilsley. It gained a hedge near Warren Farm, but was a rough way, now wide, now narrow, among the hazel, brier, elder, and nettle. Sometimes there was an ash in the hedge, and once a line of spindly elms followed it round a curve. It was high, but not yet free among these hedges. Then it descended, deeply worn and rough, to where a signpost marked roads to Aldworth and Compton on the left, Cholsey and Wallingford on the right. Then all was open country, mostly turf, carved by many trackways and with trees, as a rule, only to shelter the thatched, solitary farm-house and barns, or to make a clump and landmark at a summit where there was a tumulus, as on Churn Hill. The road was scattered in pieces over the open turf among thorn bushes and alongside a Scotch fir clump, as it went down towards Churn station. These tracks were green with a central white one, and that had green banks and a few thorns. On reaching the road from Moulsford to East Ilsley my way seemed to be continued by one passing Chance Farm and keeping on the north side of the hills through an uninhabited hollow among downs which are bare of everything but grass, Churn railway station, and a farm, except when dotted with soldiers' tents. But there was now a little to the south of this a clear and unbroken high ridge extending westwards into Wiltshire, and this the Ridgeway undoubtedly followed: only the connection between my way over Roden Downs and the higher ridge was no longer a direct one. The connecting road was that from Moulsford to Ilsley, and along it I had to turn round west and even south to gain the ridge, where the Ridgeway left it at right angles to go north-west. Hedges no longer bounded either side of the broad turf track. It was as free as the blue paths in the snowy heavens. It looked down upon everything but the clouds, and not seldom on them in the early morning or in rain. On its left the downward slope was broken and very gradual, so that it was far rarer to see a church tower like Ilsley within a mile than a ridge of woods five miles off or a bare range that might be twenty. It was already higher than the Icknield Way at Telegraph Hill; it had climbed out of choice, and it would descend only of necessity. On its right the slope was far steeper, and sometimes a little way from the foot lay the villages; sometimes the land rose again in several rolls this way and that, and the nearest village would be beyond the last of them, three or four miles away. Either corn or pure turf and scattered furze lay about the road. One piece of furze was called "Poor's Furze," and what is more, the poor were gathering it for fuel though it was Midsummer: tall rye came up to the edge of it.

Now the Ridgeway had risen up to its perfect freedom, away from the river and the low land, from the glaring roads and the collections of houses.

This way men of old came of necessity ; yet I found it hard not to think now that the road was thus climbing to heights of speculation, to places suited for exploring the ridges and solitudes of the spirit ; it seemed in one mood a hermit road going out into the wilderness to meditate and be in lifelong retirement ; in another mood a road for the young, eager warrior or reformer going up and away for a time from cloying companions to renew his mighty youth.

I saw, however, more racehorses than confirmed hermits or aspiring warriors or reformers. Before it was ordained that cricket should be played on billiard tables, there were a pitch and a pavilion here beside the Ridgeway near the Abingdon road. Elevens drove up from Oxford, and a cheerful scene it was, albeit nobody's fortune was made. It was too good and rustic a custom not to decay. After that, they say, the pavilion became an early-morning rendezvous for men with lurchers after the hares, a refuge for belated soldiers, a convenience for several breeds of idlers, philosophers, and adventurers. These it was decided to centralize as much as possible in prisons, workhouses, lunatic asylums, cemeteries, town "rookeries," and the like. The pavilion thus became useless and was pulled down. Nevertheless, there it is, still very clear in a number of aging heads. So far as I could learn, it was the nearest approach to a permanent hermitage on the ridge of these downs. In their season there are shepherds' shelters, and caravans for the steam-plough men or for persons engaged in the writing of books ; but nothing permanent except Wayland's Smithy.

Suppose a philosopher were to live in and about these old stones, for a year or two he might be quite undisturbed. Then he would be arrested on suspicion after some crime. A ploughman would reveal that he had seen the man about. It would reach a pressman with a camera. He would get somebody to pose either in Wayland's Smithy or a similar place at Wimbledon or Balham. A column about "the simple life" would be printed in a newspaper illustrated by these photographs. By this time the real philosopher, a hairy and uncommunicative man, would have been released. A rival pressman would travel to Wantage Road with a third-class ticket, which he would call either second or first class in his list of expenses. He would assail the philosopher, and with as much grace as is compatible with haste and a preoccupied mind, would bid him describe his experiences in answer to well-chosen leading questions. The philosopher might possibly fail to understand the pressman's object, or even his English ; he might seem to refuse. Then the other would produce his card, claiming instant attention as the representative of both the *Hourly Deceiver* and the *Evening Tinkle-Tinkle*. This would amuse, puzzle, or infuriate the hairy man. His laughter or his anger would be mistaken for rudeness. The pressman would return to Wantage Road and in the train invent far better things than ever were on sea or land, and he would have no difficulty in illustrating his article by photographs

Wayland's Smithy.

which the philosopher would never see. But the people of the neighbourhood would see. Then boys would go up on a Sunday afternoon and stare and perhaps trample down the wheat. A town councillor or a retired missionary or other man of culture would inspect the scene. In the philosopher's absence it would be discovered that Wayland's Smithy was undrained and improperly ventilated. A woman would be scared at a distant view of the philosopher. It would be time for something to be done. Then one of two things would happen. Either the man would disappear as quietly as mist or as last year's books: or he would be told to go, roused to eloquence or violence, arrested and imprisoned, and his story told in twenty lines in the local papers. From time to time the police of neighbouring counties would torment him until at last he could be certified as a lunatic. Instead of giving him a large plate of ham and eggs, followed by apple dumplings and then prussic acid, they would shut him up for ever in a building with innumerable windows, from any of which he could look out and see lunatics. Nevertheless, he would have had that one year unmolested at Wayland's Smithy.

This, however, is only a possibility comparatively picturesque. The real thing was less amusing, and the scene of it was not Wayland's Smithy but Lone Barn. That winter a man might have picked up the paper after breakfast and found descriptions of funerals and marriages, the well-attended presentation to the local member of Parliament, the successful meeting of his rival, the list of hunting appointments, and a column and a half headed, "Suffering Children—Parental Neglect—Queer Defence—Severe Sentences—Magistrate's Scathing Condemnation." A capital fox-hunter presiding, the bench had given four months' hard labour to a man and wife for neglecting their seven young children "in such a way as to cause them unnecessary suffering and injury to their health." Having scorched his back parts the reader would turn his front parts to the fire and read on. These nine had been living for some weeks at Lone Barn, which lies unexpectedly in a small hollow at one of the highest points of the downs, three miles from the nearest hamlet. It had long been deserted. The farm-house was ruinous, and a fox taking refuge there could not be dislodged from the fallen masonry and elder and yew tree roots. The hunters had noticed nothing in the barn.

I knew the farm-house and had often wondered about the man who built it in that solitude somewhere in the eighteenth century. It had walls of unusual thickness, such as could not have been overthrown simply by time and weather. It must long have been empty and subject to the hostility of discontented spirits such as probably infest a house, as they do a man, left utterly alone. I had not suspected that anybody was living in the barn, but I remember a pale, shuffling man carrying a child who begged from me monotonously as I came down the hill in mist a little before dark. I had given him something without exactly realizing that he was a man, so frail, subdued, and weak-voiced had he been—a creation of the mist quite in harmony with the hour. This was probably Arthur Aubrey Bishopstone, who was now in prison.

He and his wife and six children had arrived at the barn on Christmas Eve. For a week before they had been at a barn nearer the village, but as this had to be repaired they were turned out. They were allowed to settle in Lone Barn because Bishopstone had done an occasional day's work for the farmer on whose land it stood. During January and February he did several more days' work. The wife and children remained in the barn. The two eldest had measles, the sixth had pneumonia ; all were verminous. On Christmas Day a seventh had been born in Lone Barn. The mother, who had fainted in court a week before and had been remanded, pleaded guilty of neglect, but said that "she could not do in a barn as she could in a cottage," there being no bed, no furniture, and no water except from a cattle pond half a mile away. The man had been unable to get a cottage. The family had been found lying round a fire in the barn, and after medical examination arrested. Bishopstone hardly spoke in answer to the questions and insults of the bench, but he was understood to say, " The Lord is on my side," and several other blasphemous or unintelligible things, which were no defence or excuse. The nine were now condemned to the comfort of the workhouse and the prison until haymaking time.

I went to Lone Barn again, the birthplace of Francis Albert Edward Bishopstone.

The black brook, full of the white reflections of its snowy banks and beginning to steam in the sun, was hourly growing and coiling all its long loops joyously through the land. The dabchick was laughing its long shrill titter under the alder roots. Faint, soft shadows fell on to the snow from the oaks, whose grey skeletons were outlined in snow against the clear deep blue of the now dazzling sky. Thrushes were beginning to sing, as if it had always been warm and bright. In hedge and thicket and tall wood, myriads of drops were falling and singing in the still air. Against the south the smooth downs were white under a diaphanous haze of grey, and upon them seemed to rest heavenly white mountains, very still, dream-like, and gently luminous. Lone Barn lay up in the haze invisible.

At the foot of the hills the land was divided by low hedges into broad fields. There no birds sang and no stream gurgled. The air was full of the pitiful cries of young lambs at their staggering play in the shallow snow. One ewe stood with her new-born lamb in a stamped, muddy circle tinged with blood amidst the pure white. The lamb was yellowish green in colour; it stumbled at her teats, fell down and sucked upon its knees. The big mother stood still, shaggy, stubborn, meek, with her head down, her eyes upon me, her whole nature upon the lamb buried in her wool, part of her.

The hill was hedgeless save where a narrow, ancient road deeply trenched it in ascending curves, lined by thorns. The road had probably not been trodden since that procession of ten had descended towards the town six miles away. A kestrel had killed a gold-crest upon the bank, and as I approached it sailed away from the crimson-centred circle of feathers on the snow. But the wind had been the chief inhabitant of the slopes, and unseen of mortal eyes it had been luxuriously, playfully carving the snow which submerged the hedge. The curved wind-work in the drift, deeply ploughed or deliberately chiselled, remained in the stillness as a record of the pure joy of free, active life contented with itself. It was the same blithe hand which had shaped the infant born in this black barn.

An old plum tree, planted when barn and house were built, and now dead and barkless, stood against one end, and up it had climbed a thick ivy stem that linked barn and tree inseparably with a profusion of foliage, emerald and white. The last of its doors lay just outside in the dead embers of the tramps' fire. Thus open on both sides to the snow-light and the air the barn looked the work rather of nature than of man. The old thatch was grooved, riddled, and gapped, and resembled a grassy bank that has been under a flood the winter through; covered now in snow it had the outlines in miniature of the hill on which it was built. The patched walls, originally of tarred timber laid in horizontal planks, were of every hue of green and yellow that moss, lichen, and mould can bestow, each strip of board being of a different date and a different shade. What gave them something in common with one another was the fresh black stains which ran from the melting eaves to the nettle-bed below. The porches, lofty enough to admit a waggon piled as high as possible with sheaves of corn, had slipped somewhat away: it was to them alone that the exterior of the building owed a faint suggestion of a church and, consequently, a pathetic, undermined dignity: without them it would have seemed wholly restored to nature, amiably and submissively ruinous, with a silence in which not the most perverse mind could have detected melancholy. But within it was unexpectedly lofty, and the ponderous open timber-work, rough-hewn and naturally curved, was obviously performing too efficiently the task of supporting the roof: it at once inspired the thought that it should ere now have relaxed the strain of its crooked arms and acquiesced and slipped or collapsed. The oak floor was pierced in many places by wear and by drippings from the broken roof; grass and corn had grown up through the crevices and died. Some of the fallen thatch had been piled in a dry corner for a bed. In the centre of the floor was another sign of its late use—squares chalked by the children for the playing of a game. I walked to and fro. There were no ghosts, or so it seemed.

A starved thrush lay dead in a corner. That was all. I stirred the bed with my stick, meaning to set fire to it. An old coat was concealed beneath it, and out of the pocket fell a book.

On the front page was written, "A. A. Bishopstone, —— College, Oxford, October, 1890." The first pages were filled with accounts of expenditure, subscriptions, purchases, etc., the items abbreviated as a rule beyond recognition. Apparently he had soon ceased to keep accounts. Several pages were torn out and a mere few left only to save their other halves farther on. The book had then begun to serve another purpose. Under the date March, 1891, there was a list of books read during the term ending in that month—"*The Letters of Flaubert*, Gilchrist's *Blake*, etc." He had meant to make a comment on this reading, perhaps, but it was crossed out deliberately lest he should be tempted to decipher the hateful thing. He had left only the words, "It is a mistake to leave comments of this kind on record, as in after years one is unable to get back at their meaning and the imperfectly expressive words are irritating and humiliate. The mere names of books read, people seen, places walked to and the like are more eloquent far. This day I have burnt my old diaries. They help the past to haunt us out of its grave." Consequently there were from time to time carelessly written jottings of names of books, lists of places visited with dates: they were eloquent enough. On some pages short poems and passages of prose were copied out in a very neat hand, showing a kind of priestly sense of reverence for Claudian's poem *On the Sirens*, etc. These entries needed no comment, the serious worship implied in the caligraphy was unmistakable; Bishopstone would have no difficulty in recalling to his mind the mood in which they were copied out. They were headed usually by no more than the year in which they were written down, sometimes not at all. Thus he wrote "1892" at the head of a page and apparently added nothing, for it was in an altered hand that the prayer from Shelley was copied :—

Make me thy lyre even as the forest is.

Next, in March of the same year, he had written down, perhaps from dictation, the names of historical books, with a few words showing that in the following summer he would have to go up for the examination which had qualified him for a degree. Evidently he was resolved to work hard at special books and to put behind him the intellectual luxuries of Rabelais, etc. Whether he read too hard or not is uncertain, but the entry for September of that year was merely, " Brain fever and a 2nd class. I am now alone."

The next entry was in 1893 : " Sell all thou hast and follow Me." In the same year came the words : " I possess my working clothes and a Greek testament. I earn 14s. a week."

There was no more for that year, but under 1894 were a number of detached thoughts, such as :—

" 'All men are equal' is only a corollary of 'All men are different'—if only the former had been forgot instead of latter. It might have changed things less—and more."

" Forgive we one another, for we know not what we do.

" Each man suffers for the whole world and the whole world for each man. There is little distinction between the destinies of one man and another if this is understood.

"Let us not exalt worldly distinctions, titles, etc., by saying that they make no difference."

In 1895 came the words, "East Anglia—the Fens—Yorkshire—the Lakes," and the isolated thought:

"To be alone in eternity is the human lot of a man, but to be alone in time, alas! alas!"

The next year he had not touched the book: it was the year of his marriage, for in 1897 he had written: "We have now been married one year." A list of villages followed showing a zigzag course right across England; then the thought: "There is nothing like the *visible* solitude of another soul to teach us our own. Two hungers, two thirsts, two solitudes, begetting others."

Was it perhaps at the birth of a child—the date is not given, it might have been the same year, 1897—that he wrote this? "To him who is born into eternity it matters little what happens in time, and a generation of pain is as the falling of a leaf." Then:—

"Unhappiness is apart from pain. When they tell us that in the Middle Ages and even in the last century men suffered more pain and discomfort than we, they do not tell us that they also had less unhappiness. Many a battlefield has seen more joy than pain; many a festival as little of either."

And then, on a page to itself:—

"We are looking for straight oak sticks in a world where it is hazel that grows straight."

That he was still travelling was indicated only by names of places written down without comment. A week's accounts showed the expenditure of 10s.

on the food of himself, his wife, and John and Paul, two children. In March, 1898, he wrote :—

"The road northward out of Arundel leads to Heaven"; to which he had added, "So does Lavender Hill."

Other thoughts were set down in the same year :

"The man who is discontented with this world is like a blackbird who desires to be a plover that calls by night in the wandering sky.

"To have loved truly, be it for an hour only, is to be sure of eternity. Love is eternity. And if we have not loved, then also we are destined to eternity in order that in some other condition we may yet love.

"If only we did not *know* that in this world it is often well to attempt what it would not be well to achieve.

"Preach extravagance and extremes and ideals that haply we may achieve something above mediocrity. If we preach compromise we may not achieve more than desolation. And yet even out of desolation may bloom the rose.

"Exactly the same proportion of marriages as of illicit unions are immoral, even in a worldly sense."

In 1899 it must have been the death of a child that dictated the words :—

"I do not shed tears : I did that when she was born, for I saw her lie dead in the cot where she smiled."

There was a long interval and then one short entry :—

"I possess everything, but in the world's sense

nothing but my name—A. A. B.; if I could lose that I should be a better citizen, not of the world, but of the universe of eternity. Are the stars called Procion and Lyra except by astronomers? Then why should I have a name?—unless, indeed, there were a name which described me as a poem describes an emotion. I will be nameless. I will no longer condemn myself to this title of A. A. B."

The next and final entries all belonged to the winter which he spent in the barn.

On Christmas Eve :—

"Life will never be better or nobler, nor has ever been, than here at this instant in my breast. But—may I never be content to know it lest to-morrow and to-morrow and to-morrow be the less for it."

Then :—

"What is man? One moment he is a prayer, another a flower of God, another a flame to consume he knows not what save that it is himself. And, again, he is but a dungeon in which an infant's cry is echoing. One day I saw soldiers, and I was nothing but, as it were, a sea-shell to record the clattering hoofs, the scarlet, the shattering trumpet.

"The children have a doll that was given to them. They are talking to it and about it—as I talk to and about another man.

"I heard the wind rustle in the dead leaves this morning, I heard it rustle over my grave, and over the world's, and over the embers of all the stars, and I was not afraid.

"What name has my beautiful barn in heaven? In it was born a man in the sight of his brothers and sisters. God has told me my seed shall be multiplied as the sands of the sea. Can it be that out of this barn will grow the regeneration of the world, or will the forgotten memory of it trouble the well-being of some citizen far hence in time and so give birth to a flame, a prayer, a rose out of the soul of him ? It is cold, yes, but the frost is one of the angels.

"A doctor has been here, a man not used to our life. He too felt that it was cold. He said that little Francis—whom Mary calls Albert Edward—is ill and may die. If he does, then it may be from the corpse of an infant the saviour of society will be born."

These were the last words. On the day after the doctor's visit the arrest was made. Arthur Aubrey Bishopstone and two of the children died in the infirmary of the prison. Francis Albert Edward, born at Lone Barn on Christmas Day, recovered from the effects of his birth and left the workhouse at the end of June with his mother and four brothers. I believe that after Lone Barn there was nothing they missed less than Arthur Aubrey Bishopstone. If they had been given to considering such matters, they would have said that he ought to have lived solitary and let his hair grow in Wayland's Smithy instead of marrying and begetting seven children, of whom only two were able to die in infancy.

Lone Barn has since been burnt to the ground, and should Francis Albert Edward (his real name) or the world visit the scene of his nativity, to worship or verify the facts, they would find in that hollow of the downs only a square space of nettles, poppies, and bachelor's buttons, amidst the turf. . . .

Coming to the telegraph posts of Abingdon Lane —the Abingdon and Newbury road—the turf was furrowed this way and that. Gorse and thorn, surrounding the crossing of the straight, white road and the green way, made a frame as for some wayside event of no common kind, such as the birth of Francis; but the sun shone and the wind blew and betrayed nothing. Then the road was a central track of very little rutted turf, and flowers and long grass on either side; it had banks, but no thorns growing on them. The valley was beautiful, the mile-distant tedded hay looking like sea sand, the elms very dark in their lines or masses above the green corn, the villages hidden and the single farm-houses dim among trees, and the land rising beyond to a ridge saddled here and there with dark clumps on the horizon. In one place a far-off upland of newly ploughed chalk was almost snowy in misty whiteness. The clouds of the sky and the hot mist of earth dimmed the pale ploughland and the corn until the trees appeared to be floating on them as on a sea. They were cutting hay a little way off to my left, and as the horses and the mowing-machine came into sight at some speed it seemed to me that but for the seat it was probably much like a British war chariot. To the right the slope of the down was turf. Sometimes the road had a bank on each side, sometimes only on one; near the crossing of the road to East Hendred it was for a time without a bank; in other places the ditch was clearer than the bank. There was corn with its poppies, white campions, and charlock on the right, hay on the left. Woods, now on the left and now on the right, sometimes touched the road; but they never reached it from both sides at once —it never passed through a wood. In one of the roadside woods on the left a great tumulus stood disembowelled among the beeches: this was Scutchamer Knob on Cuckhamsley Hill—or, as I have heard it called, "Scotchman's Hob." This name an old carter had apparently justified to himself in part by the fact that an old road coming from the north—perchance from Scotland—passes close by, namely Hungerford Lane, which has a separate existence from Milton Hill near Steventon to Land's End on Knoll End Down near Farnborough.

Above Lockinge Park the road was about forty yards wide of level turf, between a bank and fence on the right and a natural low wall of turf above it on the left. But the new reservoir, the new plantation of firs and their iron fences, at this point might have persuaded the traveller that Lockinge Park was going to absorb the Ridgeway as it did the Icknield Way two centuries ago. At a very high point near by was a slender white column and cross upon a mound of turf erected in memory of Robert Loyd Lindsay, Baron Wantage, by his wife. The road went lightly away from this over the bare turf, having on its left the thorny slopes of Yew Down and on the right a sunken tumulus. Several deep tracks descended towards Lockinge, and at a tumulus beyond the first road to Wantage a branch entered on the left from Farnborough exactly like the main track—if it can be called a branch that was itself a parish boundary and gave its course to the main track for some distance. This tumulus formed part of the right bank of the Ridgeway.

I noticed that I seldom did more than glance at the country southward on my left. The steep downward slope that was never far off on the right, the wide vale below and the very distant hills sometimes visible beyond, could always draw my eyes from the south. On that side there was a beautiful region falling and then rising again to a height not much lower than the Ridgeway, and crowned with trees at the top of the rise, as e.g. beyond Fawley. There were several rough, thorny slopes on that side, each thorn distinct ; and these are peculiarly attractive. Yet I could not look at them long. It was the same when I walked back in the opposite direction. The vale spread out in the north was satisfying, and the horizon was distant enough to quiet if it ever awakened desire : I never wished to descend. The two or three miles of country visible in the south was far more positively attractive, as well as by chance less known to me. Perhaps the horizon was too near and was soon merely tantalizing : certainly it gave no rest. Also the land fell away very little before rising again to this horizon, and consequently gave none of the pleasure of a low and, as it were, subject landscape. The scene awakened desire, but I could not turn aside to satisfy it. Therefore, perhaps, since it could not be satisfied and stilled as by the distant northern horizon, I turned away.

The road was going broad and green and straight between bare banks in the course set by the tributary from Farnborough, when suddenly it bent to the south for a few yards, and then again west by a little pond under some willows. It descended, much narrowed and hedged, past the ash trees and

Letcombe Castle.

sycamores of White House, and then, with a sharp northward turn along the Wantage road and in a few yards another to the west at Red House, it recovered its direction and presumably its original course. Probably the half a mile or more between the two crooks is not an innovation, but the crooks themselves are, as it were, the punishment inflicted on the old road by two newer or at some time more vigorous roads cutting across it.

Beyond Red House I passed Letcombe Castle or

Segsbury Camp, the road running close and parallel to its straight south side. A road crossed mine and penetrated the green ramparts of the camp from a corrugated-iron farm that stood with a thatched barn under some ash trees—behind it a grassy down with clumps beyond. The road was now so broad that it was hardly at all marked except downhill, or where a crossway roughened it, or at some busy section between one cross-road and another, where it would have one narrow, well-worn strip. At the right-hand turning to Letcombe Bassett stood a sycamore and some ash trees, and there were roses in the thorn hedge. Letcombe Bassett was at the foot of a round buttress of the downs called Gramp's Hill, but was half hidden in grouped trees which continued above and alongside the winding white road to Letcombe Regis a mile beyond. Gramp's Hill and the next and far more prominent hill formed between them a long, deep hollow, winding up into the hill and terraced on its slopes with flights of green steps. This winding made almost an island of a small hill, round and flat-topped, and the top of this hill had been mown and a waggon in the centre was being loaded with hay. Here was the place to build a castle in the air—and also on the turf of the downs. The man who did so would probably inhabit somewhat longer than the philosopher did Wayland's Smithy. He might live there even until he died. But it is not likely that his heir—supposing that he had an heir—would continue after him. In any case it would at once be called the "Folly." Clumps of trees planted on high places to please the eye and to be a landmark are now called "Follies" almost as a matter of course. Any house built high or in a great solitude is likely to be called a "Folly." A house may earn the name by having walls more than a foot thick, in a district of jerry-builders where builders are bankrupt once a month. Thus people condemn the extraordinary. If it is a little thing like a white blackbird, they shoot at it: if it is a big, helpless thing like a whale stranded in Cornwall, they carve it alive. But to call it a "Folly" and have done with it is the most innocent form of condemnation. In fact, it is by this time rather venerably pretty. They call the far-seen clump of beeches on Liddington Hill the "Folly"; the clump a quarter-mile north-west of Wayland's Smithy is Odstone Folly; Ashbury Folly is the clump at the crossing over the Ridgeway down to Ashbury Church. They call a house a "Folly" with less benevolence. They see—or they feel—in the strange, high, or solitary situation part of an attempt to mould the course and conditions of life, or to escape from them. They see—or they dimly imagine—a being who is trying to make his, or some woman's, like a poem, or like a work of art—

> Carved with figures strange and sweet,
> All made out of the carver's brain. . . .

It is not that they see the blasphemy of it like that of Babel or of the Titans. But they know that the builders of Babel and the Titans will fail, and if they cannot beat them themselves they will be on the side of the one who can. I should myself be sorry to see a house—such a one as is likely to be built—on that island between Gramp's and Hackpen hills. But if it were such a house as Morgan's Folly! I warmed with the thought of transporting that hill-top tower to this peninsulated table of turf, by the expenditure of a sum sufficient to have given a free library to Letcombe Bassett.

I do not know if it was called a Folly, but there was a plantation at the cross-road from Sparsholt to Lambourn which I liked—a long, narrow plantation of beeches close together alongside the cross-road and touching the Ridgeway on one side; on the other was a tumulus. Here it was a broad road with no hedges, there being corn on the right, and sheep, enclosed by a wire fencing, on the left. It was now near its highest point, nearly eight hundred feet, at the Hill Barn that stands with its company of stacks amidst a group of ash trees above Sparsholt. The purple meadow crane's-bill was growing beside the road near Hill Barn.

I left the Ridgeway that morning by the Blowing-stone Hill and its woods, and went to Sparsholt, which has a quarter-mile of chestnut and lime, and then beech and elm shadow on the road to its church. One bee was buzzing inside as I walked over the stones and brasses of the floor and looked at the Commandments, the Creed, the Lord's Prayer, and the royal arms, on the wall, but chiefly at three recumbent stone effigies lying asleep and private within a chapel, guarded by stone lions, railings, and a locked gate.

CHAPTER X

EIGHTH DAY—SPARSHOLT TO TOTTERDOWN, ON THE RIDGEWAY, BY WHITE HORSE HILL AND WAYLAND'S SMITHY

I WAS going through Sparsholt the next day just after the children had gone into school after their mid-morning play. The road was quieter than the church on that hot, bright morning. As I walked under the garden trees I came slowly within hearing of a melody played so lightly, or so far lost among winds or leaves, that I could hardly distinguish it. It was an hour when nearly everyone is at work. A poor, ragged girl was walking in front of me in awkward haste. But she stopped at the same time as I did, to listen. The music was not everything. The shadow and the filtered light, the silence of the music half submerged, the busy hour so steeped in tranquillity, helped the player to express perfect carelessness and freedom from the conditions of life—summer, wealth, luxury, happiness, youth, gaiety, innocence, and benevolence. They expressed it for us, as that river-side garden picture at Watlington doubtless expressed it for others. But presently the player lighted upon a melody which took me right away from Sparsholt and the summer morning and the tranquillity. I could not catch every note, but even the fragmentary skeleton of "Caradoc's Hunt" could not be mistaken. At a first hearing this old hunting song seemed to be much the same thing as Scott's

Waken, lords and ladies gay,

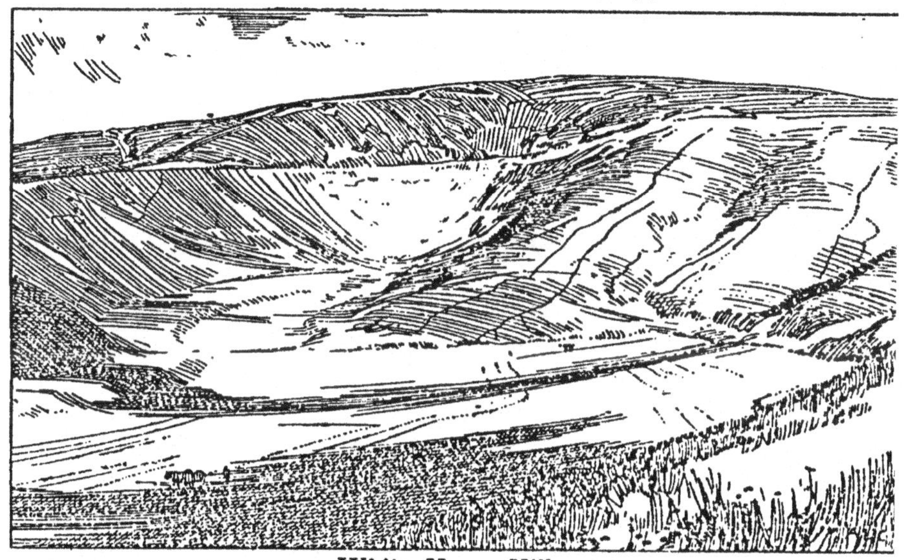

White Horse Hill.

and little more than the north countryman's

One morning last winter to Holm Bank there came
A noble brave sportsman, Squire Sandys was his name.

Many have heard it and thought it just one of the best, perhaps the princeliest, of hunting songs. With a little change it might have been a battle song; for it was martial and high-tempered, and would launch cavalry as well as huntsmen. It was a little too nervously quick and dancing for a battle song; such pace, such height of spirit could not endure. Yet the trumpets before a charge have often brought the song into the hearts of young soldiers, and their chargers and they have done extravagant things for the gay tune's sake. It suggested the haughtiness and celerity of youth, audacious and fantastic pleasures, voices of command and laughter, many-coloured and all splendid dresses, neighing and prancing horses, hounds lazily quarrelling in the sun, gallant March weather. The gates of a castle stood all wide open for the first time since the beginning of winter, and arrowy winds and humid fragrance were invading the stale shadows. As the first flowers break out of the old, dark earth, so the youths and maidens with their purple and gold, green and white, broke out of this old, dark castle upon the Welsh moorland. The sharp horse-shoes trampled the first green of spring and the first yellow blossoms, even as the riders would trample the hearts of men and women, and as freely upon their own hearts, their own strength and health and happiness. The sunlight played like a thousand sprites, on rippling waters, on the gold and silver ornaments of riders and horses, on horns of gold. Bright as the sun, clear as the west wind, joyous as the heart of man and hound and horse sounded the horns.

There was nothing more in the three verses, there seemed little more in the melody. After a little talk and much laughter and shouting with deep and shrill voices, blowing of horns, cheering, and chiding of steeds, summoning and urging of hounds, they rode away. They climbed the wild hills and saw an angry sea of yet wilder hills in the distance. They descended into the rich vales. They scattered joyfully. They gathered together as joyfully. They feasted until better than any wit or beauty or adventure seemed sleep. Then they slept.

Other listeners to the song might think rather of a later hunt assembling before a cheerful Georgian mansion with many windows, and behind one of them a lady playing " Caradoc's Hunt " on a spinet, and warbling it in Saxon. I thought of such a one as I heard the invisible lady playing at Sparsholt.

Others, again, would be content with nothing later than the age of chivalry and the *Mabinogion.* The hunters would all be auburn or yellow-haired young men. They are clad in yellow tunics, green hose, and shoes of parti-coloured leather clasped at the instep with gold. Some carry bows of ivory strung with deer sinews, the shafts of whalebone headed with gold and winged with peacock's feathers. Others have silver-headed spears of ash-wood coloured azure. All wear whalebone-hafted and gold-hilted daggers and horns of ivory. Their hunting is earnest, though elaborated with much decoration of custom, style, and ceremony. They are men who must go hungry but for the chase. They run or ride to hunt the stag or the boar, and nobly beautiful and blithe look they as they begin to move away from the castle, and their tall, brindled white-breasted greyhounds, wearing collars of rubies, are sporting like sea-swallows from side to side of them. But they may encounter foes instead of quarry; they may kill or be killed by young braves from other borders. So with all the gallantry of dress and harping there is something grim in their going forth; nor is it idle bombast for one among them to ride out carrying only what he calls the mightiest of all weapons—the harp—on which he plays "Caradoc's Hunt" at the starting.

These things and others, according to the singer and the hearer, the song readily suggested. But they are mistaken who are contented by these suggestions, sufficient as they are for a warm summer's morning in a green lane. They are deceived by the qualities which "Caradoc's Hunt" has in common with other hunting songs, especially by the galloping rhythm and the notes like a challenge of horns. Even when that boastful riding harper played it the tune was old. He was a bard, and though he played it for the young hunters for the flashes of gaiety and mettle upon its surface, it intrigued his own heart with a rich mystery of antiquity. Already legend as well as the bards and harpers had begun to play with the melody. It was said, for example, to have been the favourite hunting song of the "Lady of the Night" in her earthly days, and even that she sang it, or had it sung and harped to her, now that she was an inhabitant of night and the underworld. Solitary, benighted peasants or travellers saw her black hair streaming over her green vest and crimson mantle as she galloped fiercely over the mountains or in the heavens. Her horse was white. She hallooed as she rode in a wild voice, at times harsh and abrupt like a heron's, at others clear and laughing like a wood-owl's. The hounds streamed after her, howling in tumultuous chorus, and the sound grew louder as the pack raced farther and farther away. They were the hounds of the underworld. They followed her in a stream or fan as closely as if the foremost held the tip of her mantle. In some packs the hounds were small, and were white all over except the shells of their ears, which were rose-coloured; and they had eyes like lighted pearls. Some were black with red spots, others red with black spots. There were also hounds all blood-red, with eyes of flame. They hunted the spirits of men destined to die soon, or of the dead who were unfit either for heaven or for hell. They prophesied deaths and calamity. However fierce, they were always even frantically joyous, but some thought the hallooing of the lady was often close to lamentation. Only when the sound of "Caradoc's Hunt" was heard was she as joyous as her hounds. Her sadness made it believed in places that she was no huntress at all, but the quarry, or at least that she hunted for a punishment, that she was doomed by god or devil thus to flee all night through cloudland or the most desert regions of earth. Hunting or hunted, it was certain that she was powerless to change her fate. Hunting was what she most loved on earth. Perhaps she still loved it, or she was being punished for the crime of pride or immoderate love of the chase. One story was that she had been very beautiful and vain of her beauty, and on her death-bed had exacted a promise to bury her in her most radiant apparel. Another story, more venerable, was that she had so loved hunting as to cry out once in a strong passion : " I care nothing for heaven if I cannot hunt there." When she died, therefore, her spirit was cursed with an everlasting compulsion to slake this most dear desire. She had to hunt eternally with the hounds of the underworld. When she heard "Caradoc's Hunt" she could not but start or follow the chase. " If I forget 'Caradoc's Hunt,' then I shall be dead indeed," she said. " I shall be quiet and sleepy as anyone else among the ghosts." When men saw her dark eyes flashing at thought of the song they could not believe that if anything of this beautiful creature was to survive the immortal remnant would not take with it " Caradoc's Hunt." She heard it at many different and some monstrous times. People thought that the tune was in her head, but she averred that she heard it outside—in the clouds or the trees or the hallooing woods—and her immediate attendants knew this to be true. She would break away from marriage or funeral to ride. She would suddenly rise up from mass to mount. She would dress at dead of night, uncouple the hounds, and hunt alone. Love, wine, sleep, religion were impotent against the melody. Everyone admitted that it was a beautiful melody ; they called it gay, or spirited, or said that it was perfectly suitable to a knightly company of riders.

This lady heard it and rode away. Hers was not the fate of the lord of Radnor Castle. He and his hounds impiously passed the night in the church of Llan-Avan, near Builth, to be near the day's coverts early; but when he rose at the dawn he found himself blinded and his hounds mad, so that he escaped only with difficulty, to earn pardon by a pilgrimage to the Holy Land. The lady's life was charmed. She rode anywhere without fear. She died young, but it was in bed. On horseback she could defy man or God.

Such was the Lady of the Night, and her legend was at least not unworthy of "Caradoc's Hunt." But as the belief in the hounds of the underworld is earlier than the Middle Ages and the ghostly hunter in darkness more venerable than the Norman lady, so is the tune. The legend might have grown to explain the tune, and it does help to illuminate the depths of which the surviving words, the mere cheerful chivalry, are no more than the glancing surface. But the tune has depth under depth, and when it is heard the plummet of the soul sinks to a profound far below the region of the lady who rides by night. What darkness the plummet fathoms, what "bottom of the monstrous world" it touches, is not to be understood. Perhaps the mystery is only that which at once haloes and enshrouds common things when we no longer feel them as common. But if at the sounding of the melody the mind's eye still sees a cavalcade of antique hunters, it is not stag or boar or questing beast that they are to follow; the castle that sends them out of its gates and may receive them at nightfall is no feudal or faery stronghold, but an image, perhaps, of the great world itself.

The Blowingstone.

But I must confess the melody did not lighten my step as I mounted again to the Ridgeway by Blowingstone Hill. The Blowingstone is a block of brown, iron-like sarsen stone standing on end, and of such a height that a man can bend over and comfortably blow into the mouthpiece at the upper side. This natural mouthpiece is the small roundish entrance to a funnel through the stone which emerges at a larger hole lower down at the back. A well-breathed person blowing bugle-fashion can make a booming that is said even now to carry five miles, if sustained for some time. At the hill-top, where it stood before it became a procurer of charity, a skilled and deep-chested hillman might have made himself heard much farther. From this hill-top, nearly seven hundred feet high, the Ridgeway rises to its greatest height. Hitherto it had hardly ever had higher land on either side of it for very many miles. At Uffington Castle it is over eight hundred feet high, but a little lower than the highest part of the camp. From the rampart about this circle of almost level turf I could see the Quarley Hill range and far over the Lambourn Downs to Martinsell Hill by Savernake; I could see Barbury Castle and the wooded hills of Clyffe and Wroughton, and Badbury, the Cotswolds, the Oxfordshire hills, Sinodun, and the Chilterns. The Dragon Hill below it is an isolated eminence shaped like the butt of an oak tree, and similar to that one in the hollow between Gramp's and Hackpen hills, but ruder and more distinct.

Past the south and lower side of Uffington Castle the Ridgeway went fairly straight, with a thorn or two on either side, towards the thick beech clump above Wayland's Smithy, sometimes a green road, sometimes worn white. The hill-side was divided among charlock and different greens in squares and triangles, and here and there a thatched barn or rick at a corner. Southward I saw the pleasant, dappled scatter of Knighton Bushes over the turf, sometimes considerable woods like those of Ashdown by Alfred's Castle; in several places the long stretch of turf reared itself up with beautiful but detached hills, like Tower Hill, as high as the main ridge. The hot, misty sun drew out all the odour from uncut grass, clover, cocks-combs, yellow bedstraw, ox-eye daisies, and bird's-foot trefoil, and the light air mixed them. Whatever was visible or hid on the left, the road always commanded the northward valley, the main expanse, and also for the most part the nearer land where the villages lay, close to the foot of the hills on which it was travelling. An enemy might have lain or moved concealed within a very short distance on the south, but never on the north, and it might be conjectured, therefore, that attack was to be feared from that side only, and that the other was friendly country to those most commonly upon the road. The camps of Lowbury, Letcombe, and Uffington were all to northward; Alfred's Castle alone was on the south, at Ashdown, among the greatest woods now surviving on this part of the Downs. It is hardly possible for unhistorically minded men to think of war on these hills, unless troops are manœuvring over them. Yet the Ridgeway is like nothing so much as a battlement walk of superhuman majesty. The hills between Streatley and Liddington form a curve in the shape of a bow, a doubly curved Cupid's bow. Following this line, always keeping at the edge of the steep northward slope and surveying the valley, the Ridgeway carries the traveller for thirty miles as if along the battlements of a castle. He begins at Streatley by having the early morning sun of spring over his right shoulder; the full light of midday is on his left as he passes Letcombe Castle; the sun is going down on his right hand as he descends to Totterdown and the pass for the Roman road and modern traffic between the hills.

It is still debated whether most or little of the downland was once covered with trees. Those recently planted on very high places have often failed to make more than a spindly and ruinous growth, as at Chanctonbury Ring, Liddington Hill, and Barbury. But wherever there is a tertiary deposit beech and oak, not to speak of lesser trees, abound and even flourish in great size and noble forms. Gorse, hawthorn, and elder rapidly take possession anywhere of neglected ground, and make an impenetrable scrub. Yews expand and beeches grow tall and close on steep and almost precipitous slopes where the chalk is easily bared by rain, traffic, or rabbits. There is thus some reason for thinking that the open downland is largely the product of cultivation and nibbling flocks.

The flocks no longer feed much on the hills, and, except when folded in squares of turnips or mustard, are seldom seen there. They have become more and more a kind of living machinery for turning vegetables into mutton, and only in their lambhood or motherhood are they obviously of a different tribe from sausage-machines, etc. In time, with the discovery of a way of concentrating food and sunlight and of adapting the organs of the sheep to these essences, it will be possible to dine carnivorously on Sunday upon what was grass on Friday; but "for ever climbing up the climbing wave," men shall sigh for lambs born filleted with a double portion of sweetbreads.

From Uffington Castle the road descended slowly, and reached six hundred feet at the Wiltshire border, a third of a mile past the road from Idstone to Ashdown. Then gradually it rose towards a point much above seven hundred feet between two distinct breasts of down south-westward. In places it had a good hedge of thorn, maple, and brier on one side, at others only isolated little thickets of thorn, brier, and black bryony, or groups where the last May-blossom met the first guelder roses. Once at a corner before Ridgeway Farm five beeches stood together making a shadow. The highest point showed me the beeches of Liddington clump, each stem distinct, the fall of clear turf down to the plain, and beyond that the Barbury clump and the long down wall bending to Avebury.

The Ridgeway was now rapidly descending, with a disused track on the left, to the gap where the Roman Ermine Street from Silchester to Gloucester, now the Swindon and Hungerford road, penetrated the hills. Without this descent from its ridge the road must have turned back so as to point almost to Streatley again, and it would have done this to avoid only about a mile of lowland before rising again to the hills which were its natural soil. Probably it did so rise, though the road called the Ridgeway in Ordnance Maps keeps to the lowland for five or six miles.

I crossed Ermine Street at Totterdown and an inn called "Shepherd's Rest," and the Ridgeway became a hard road of ordinary width between hedges and ditches. It was more like the Icknield Way than the Ridgeway, and still greater was this likeness when it reached Liddington, but made no effort to climb again to the ridges, or to keep Liddington Camp on its north side. One road does climb the ridge, going south-westward to Liddington Hill, and then south, having turned from this present road to the left at a point marked by the "Ridgeway Bush" in the time of Hoare—three-quarters of the way from Totterdown to the Swindon road. But the Ordnance Map gives the name of Ridgeway to a road going straight across the low land to Barbury, mounting the hill on the north side of that camp, and continuing along the ridge beyond Barbury to near Avebury, up over the downs again to the Avon Valley, up to Salisbury Plain, and across it, perhaps, to the Dorset coast, or skirting it to Warminster and the west. But the site of "Ridgeway Bush" is within a few yards of the westward boundary of Wanborough, and beyond Wanborough there is so far no sufficient evidence for tracing the course of the Icknield Way. The two roads came very near to one another in that parish; they may even have touched before the Ridgeway returned to its own place high up; and it is possible that as the Ridgeway in Berkshire has been mistakenly called the Icknield Way, so the lower part of what is now called the Ridgeway in Wiltshire may be the Icknield Way.

CHAPTER XI

NINTH DAY—STREATLEY TO EAST HENDRED, BY UPTON AND HAGBOURNE HILL FARM

When I started from Streatley to see the western half of the Icknield Way it was with several uncertainties. I knew that the Icknield Way was not the Ridgeway, but a lower road which was in several places not more than a mile or two away from it. This lower road, it has been said, was the Wantage-to-Reading turnpike for part at least of its course; one writer's road clearly lay south of this turnpike; another had expressed a doubt whether it was the turnpike or a road to the south. The decision that the Icknield Way in Berkshire was distinct from the Ridgeway had added this difficulty; that the Ridgeway, supposing it to have come up from the ford at Streatley, must have been a road from beyond the Thames, and what that road was I had not discovered, though it had been suggested that it was the Upper Icknield Way. But if the Icknield Way of Oxfordshire and the Icknield Way of Berkshire were linked, it must have been at Streatley, though it may also have been at other fords.

The first half-mile of the main road through Streatley to Wantage is the beginning of the Ridgeway's ascent ; but a little past the fork to Wallingford the Ridgeway becomes separate from this main road, and goes westward out of it. There

Moulsford Bottom.

was at first no possibility of an alternative out of Streatley to the west, and I set out on the same road as when I followed the Ridgeway. On my left I saw "Lyndhurst," "Bellevue," and "Montefiore," or their more expensive equivalents. I ignored the first coombe, the turning up it of the Ridgeway, and went on upon the roadside grass bordered with wormwood and traveller's joy. Almost at once the road crossed the entrance to another coombe running up westward into the Moulsford Downs, and those woods which the Ridgeway skirts on the south. It was a shallow coombe, the sides dappled with thorns, the bottom covered with corn, and in the midst of it a barn called Well Barn. Through the mouth of the coombe which opened towards the river in the east I saw the pale corn, and the dark woods above it, of the Chilterns. Crossing this coombe the road had no hedges, but corn on both sides. It was usually hedgeless, but banked as it went up and down, and dipped into another coombe of the same kind called Moulsford Bottom, where a quarter-mile north of the thirteenth milestone from Wantage a road came in from the South Stoke Ferry, the continuation, perhaps, of a track from the Icknield Way near Ipsden. From Moulsford Bottom the main road went visibly curving uphill, but from the top of Kingstanding Hill, at three hundred feet, it went straight between its low hedges and grassy banks towards Blewburton Hill. It had still corn on both sides in stooks, downs on the left, and on the right the valley of dark trees stretching far away into mist. It was a plain, well-kept road of easy gradients, no corners, and such banks or hedges that anything approaching in front could be seen. It lacked the company of telegraph wires.

The villages of Aston were almost completely hidden on my right, as I passed within a third of a mile of them. That was by the eleventh milestone from Wantage, and there the road was following along and under one of the low, natural walls of chalk which so often guide a road and are in turn defined by it. My road, Icknield Way or not, went hedgeless under this wall, with oats above and stubble below. The flowers on its narrow green edges were chiefly yellow parsnip and white carrot, both dear for their scents, and succory, that pale blue flower which a strange fate has closely attached to the coarsest and stiffest of dark stems and placed where dust is likely to be most thick.

Here the dust was thick, and I was glad to feel, to hear, to smell and to taste, and to see the rain falling as I passed the "Barley Mow" at Blewbury. According to custom I stood under the broad, overhanging eaves of one of Blewbury's thatched roofs and watched the rain, but it was better to be in it and to smell the wetted dust which association alone has made pleasant. Any road was good now, though mine was an unadventurous, level, probably commercial, road.

But, rain or no rain, I was looking for an excuse to leave this road at Upton, the next village, which is by the ninth milestone. The map had shown me a road, or an almost continuous line of pieces running from Upton westward to Lockinge Park, and on the east possibly connected with the roads I had already travelled between Little Stoke and Upton by way of Lollingdon Farm, Aston, and Blewbury, but traversing land near Upton which is liable to floods. Either this road or the turnpike was the Icknield Way, because a more northern road would be too low, and no more southern one had left any traces.

A hundred yards or so before the road I was on bridged the Didcot, Newbury, and Southampton Railway I noticed the line of a hedge leaving on the left at an acute angle, and forming a triangle with the railway and road for its other sides. As an old road is not likely to form such triangular fields, except with the help of a new branch, it occurred to me that this branching hedge marked an earlier or original line of the same road, or of one coming from Upton village, and there connected with the field roads from Blewbury and Aston. Across the railway another hedge and a depression that might once have been a road continued this line and led naturally into a lane turning out of the main road on the left beyond the bridge and passing Upton Vicarage. I supposed that when the railway cutting was made to have left these crossing roads in their original state would have meant making two bridges or one very broad one necessary. The courses, therefore, were slightly altered, so that, instead of a crossing or "four-went way," there was a road receiving a branch at one side of the bridge, and a second branch from an opposite direction, the left, at the other side. But on referring to the old six-inch Ordnance Map, made before the railway, I found that I was mistaken. The amended crossing may have been made when the old road was superseded by the turnpike. This left-hand road being the likely-looking road on the map, I followed it, especially as the main road, half a mile beyond, by the "Horse and Harrow," at West Hagbourne, took a right-angled turn which suggested a piecing together of two older roads, an east-and-west one and a north-and-south one.

My conjectural road began as a hedged lane that formed a short cut into the road to East Ilsley and Newbury. Crossing that road it was a cart track—with a disused, parallel course on the right—over Hagbourne Hill, past Hagbourne Hill Farm, which was derelict, but had sunflowers in the garden and ricks in the yard. Less than a furlong south of the farm is a supposed Roman burial-ground. A home-returning carter told me that the first part of the road as far as the crossing was Baits or Bates Lane. It was a cart track, or usually a strip of three or four parallel cart tracks, going parallel with the downs, and almost straight between one road and the next that came from over the downs northward to the villages. It could easily make a straight course, like all the other roads round about, because it was on an almost unbroken plateau of cornland at the foot of the downs: so level was this piece of country that in about four miles the altitudes varied only between three hundred and eighty and four hundred feet. Between me and the downs there were seldom any trees, except such few as stood by Downs Farm, its thatched barns, its old and new ricks. On the right a slight swell in the land often shut out everything but distant Oxfordshire under a blue, bulging threat of storm. The road was for the most part without hedges, and not a parish boundary. It was rarely or never sunken, but in places might have been a little embanked. On one side, shortly before reaching the Newbury road, there were two old thorns. Half a mile farther, after crossing Hungerford Lane—a track from Milton Hill to Farnborough—it had a line of elm trees on its left, which was part of the enclosure of Arfield Farm, close by. I thought Arfield—on the new one-inch Ordnance Maps spelt Aldfield—might be the same as Halvehill. The cottage pronunciation, except that it lacked an aspirate, was not discouraging. Halvehill barn was said to be on the Ickleton Street or Meer, but on inquiry I learnt that it was some way from my road down Hungerford Lane to the north, but on this side of the main road, which was here about a mile distant. This barn is now called Horn Down Barn.

Past Arfield Farm the road had hedges until it came to the tussocky little "Arfield Common," so called, but perhaps not so in fact. Here there were several forking cartways. Mine seemed to go westward along the northern hedge and its traveller's joy, but at the west side of the common, where Cow Lane comes in from Hendred, there was a gap of a hundred yards or so before the old line was taken up by a road from the south-east, which led me into the road to East Hendred. This was a little more than three miles from the beginning of the road at Upton.

As I had had as much rain as I wanted on my skin, I turned downhill under a long train of

Lombardy poplars and very lanky ash trees into East Hendred for the night. It was a thatched village built on the slopes of a little valley, its houses standing singly or in short rows high above

East Hendred.

either side of the steep streets. They stood high because the streets were very old and worn into deep hollows, and at the edges of these ran narrow, cobbled paths ; but the cottages were still higher up, and four or five stone steps led up from the paths to their doors. At the bottom stood the towered church, telling the hours and the quarters, not with clock-face and hands, but with bells. Rain, however, drowned that sweet noise in a mightier sweetness, heavy and straight rain, and no wind except what itself created. For half an hour everything—trees, mud walls, thatch, old weather-boards, pale-coloured, timbered cottages, the old chapel at a crossing railed off as a sign of private possession—everything was embedded in rain. Every sound was the rain. For example, I thought I heard bacon frying in a room near by, with a noise almost as loud as the pig made when it was stuck; but it was the rain pouring steadily off the inn roof. Then in the dripping quiet afterwards the sunset blazed in little fragments like gorgeous glass and metal betwixt the black garden foliage.

Before I went to bed an intelligent, unprejudiced man told me that the field-way I had followed was Ickleton Street or—he said it with some shyness—Ickleton Meer. I had asked no leading questions, so that his name seemed certainly the local though perhaps not invariable one. From his description and map knowledge I felt no doubt that this was the road mentioned in Wise's *Antiquities of Berkshire* (1695) as ploughed up in Wantage east field, but visible from Lockinge Park, eastward almost the whole way to Upton, through the parishes of Ardington, East Hendred, Harwell, and West Hagbourne.

It is strange that that same identification was not made in a book published in 1905. I mean Miss Eleanor G. Hayden's *Travels Round our*

Villages. She lived at West Hendred, yet described her village as lying between two roads known on the map as the " Portway " (the main road between Wantage and Reading) and Ickleton Street, adding that they were known " locally as the 'Turnpike' and the 'Ridgeway.' " Evidently she had not heard the people talk of " Ickleton Street " or " Ickleton Meer." Yet her books prove her familiar with country people and country places as are few writers of country books. Her *Travels* and her *Turnpike Travellers* and *Islands of the Vale* gave the materials for an exceptionally full picture of country life. Nothing was beneath her, and her love was equal to her curiosity. She was exceptionally modest, and put down everything with no obvious intention except fidelity to her own eyes and ears. She could be dull, and if you opened the book at random you might be disappointed ; but if you read a whole chapter you were certain to be delighted. So many books are written by bungalow countrymen that we have got used to pretty things, surprising things, pathetic things, country equivalents of the music-halls and museums of towns. There were plenty of good things in Miss Hayden's books. She was not afraid of quoting country talk at some length for its own sake, but she did not miss such things as the cottager's " strutty little hen," who was " a deal better Christ'n nor many what calls themselves sich," and the lonely shepherd's answer to the question what he and his family did without a doctor—" We just dies a nat'ral death." She appeared to make good books as others darn stockings, because of the abundant material. She gave a natural monotony and a natural charm. She showed us a village girl curtseying seven times to the crescent moon; children playing with the old mill machinery after the cheap loaf had killed it; labourers at a tug-of-war over a brook; a cavalier and lady of the old manor-house; a crossing stream, a beautiful garden, a village kitchen, a recipe for Christmas pudding and one for sloe gin, and many things from old parish accounts. But nobody bought her books. If she had given them to some journalist to mince, spice, warm, and dish up, he might have made a book of the season from them, and by now it would have been dead. Hers will last somehow or another as long as an old wall.

I lay awake listening to the rain, and at first it was as pleasant to my ear and my mind as it had long been desired; but before I fell asleep it had become a majestic and finally a terrible thing, instead of a sweet sound and symbol. It was accusing and trying me and passing judgment. Long I lay still under the sentence, listening to the rain, and then at last listening to words which seemed to be spoken by a ghostly double beside me. He was muttering: The all-night rain puts out summer like a torch. In the heavy, black rain falling straight from invisible, dark sky to invisible, dark earth the heat of summer is annihilated, the splendour is dead, the summer is gone. The midnight rain buries it away where it has buried all sound but its own. I am alone in the dark still night, and my ear listens to the rain piping in the gutters and roaring softly in the trees of the world. Even so will the rain fall darkly upon the grass over the grave when my ears can hear it no more. I have been glad of the sound of rain, and wildly sad of it in the past; but that is all over as if it had never been; my eye is dull and my heart beating evenly and quietly; I stir neither foot nor hand; I shall not be quieter when I lie under the wet grass and the rain falls, and I of less account than the grass. The summer is gone, and never can it return. There will never be any summer any more, and I am weary of everything. I stay because I am too weak to go. I crawl on because it is easier than to stop. I put my face to the window. There is nothing out there but the blackness and sound of rain. Neither when I shut my eyes can I see anything. I am alone. Once I heard through the rain a bird's questioning watery cry—once only and suddenly. It seemed content, and the solitary note brought up against me the order of nature, all its beauty, exuberance, and everlastingness like an accusation. I am not a part of nature. I am alone. There is nothing else in my world but my dead heart and brain within me and the rain without. Once there was summer, and a great heat and splendour over the earth terrified me and asked me what I could show that was worthy of such an earth. It smote and humiliated me, yet I had eyes to behold it, and I prostrated myself, and by adoration made myself worthy of the splendour. Was I not once blind to the splendour because there was something within me equal to itself? What was it? Love . . . a name! . . . a word! . . . less than the watery question of the bird out in the rain. The rain has drowned the splendour. Everything is drowned and dead, all that was once lovely and alive in the world, all that had once been alive and was memorable though dead is now dung for a future that is infinitely less than the falling dark rain. For a moment the mind's eye and ear pretend to see and hear what the eye and ear themselves once knew with delight. The rain denies. There is nothing to be seen or heard, and there never was. Memory, the last chord of the lute, is broken. The rain has been and will be for ever over the earth. There never was anything but the dark rain. Beauty and strength are as nothing to it. Eyes could not flash in it.

I have been lying dreaming until now, and now I have awakened, and there is still nothing but the rain. I am alone. The unborn is not more weak or more ignorant, and like the unborn I wait and wait, knowing neither what has been nor what is to come, because of the rain, which is, has been, and must be. The house is still and silent, and those small noises that make me start are only the imagination of the spirit or they are the rain. There is only the rain for it to feed on and to crawl in. The rain swallows it up as the sea does its own foam. I will lie still and stretch out my body and close my eyes. My breath is all that has been spared by the rain, and that comes softly and at long intervals, as if it were trying to hide itself from the rain. I feel that I am so little I have crept away into a corner and been forgotten by the rain. All else has perished except me and the rain. There is no room for anything in the world but the rain. It alone is great and strong. It alone knows joy. It chants monotonous praise of the order of nature, which I have disobeyed or slipped out of. I have done evilly and weakly, and I have left undone. Fool! you never were alive. Lie still. Stretch out yourself like foam on a wave, and think no more of good or evil. There was no good and no evil. There was life and there was death, and you chose. Now there is neither life nor death, but only the rain. Sleep as all things, past, present, and future, lie still and sleep, except the rain, the heavy, black rain falling straight through the air that was once a sea of life. That was a dream only. The truth is that the rain falls for ever and I am melting into it. Black and monotonously sounding is the midnight and solitude of the rain. In a little while or in an age—for it is all one—I shall know the full truth of the words I used to love, I knew not why, in my days of nature, in the days before the rain: "Blessed are the dead that the rain rains on."

CHAPTER XII

TENTH DAY—EAST HENDRED TO WANBOROUGH, BY LOCKINGE PARK, WANTAGE, ASHBURY, AND BISHOPSTONE

On the following morning early I returned to where I had left my conjectured road, which I shall now call Ickleton Street, at the crossing half a mile south of East Hendred Church. The eastern road at the crossing came from the south-east (out of Hungerford Lane) and was only for a few hundred yards in the line of Ickleton Street, falling into it a hundred yards or so west of Aldfield Common, where I had lost the road. The western road was apparently mine, but it was so unimportant for *through* traffic that though the eastern road forked on entering the northern or Hendred road, neither of the forks ran exactly into Ickleton Street. Between these forks was a triangular waste of yellow parsnip, wild carrot, and dock, uneven from digging, and somewhat above the roads which were sunken by downhill wearing.

Ickleton Street ran for a third of a mile straight westward to a cross-track at the East and West Hendred boundary. It was hedgeless as before, and being on a slight depression the horizon was often a very near one of corn, topped by a distant bright cloud or cloud-shaped dark clump of beech. At this cross-track I had to turn a few yards south and then westward along a track of the same kind. Not being sunk, or raised, or hedged, or banked, or ditched, the road could be ploughed up easily and its course slightly changed, as here, to serve a barn. This was Tames Barn, a thatched quadrangle of new ricks and old barns and sheds built of boards now heavily lichened. Past the barn it went as before, flat and hard-beaten, with broad ruts, and a slight dip on the right side—a wall not half as deep as the corn was high ; there were a few blackthorns on this side. On the left sheep were folded in clover. Ahead the Lockinge Woods showed their tops between the rounds of Roundabout Hill, which was newly reaped, and Goldbury Hill, which was part stubble, part aftermath. At the first turning to West Hendred, which made the road crook a little to the south—and in this crook—there were two or three rough sarsens, iron-coloured but blotched with orange and dull silver, lying deep in the grass. A little way back I had noticed another on the left, and there was another, I think, east of Arfield Farm, beside the track.

Past the second turning to West Hendred (from East Ginge) the tiny dip or wall below the right side of the road became a pleasant, high, green wall with blackthorns and elders on it, and the road was a green one, flowery with scabious, and had a bank above it, with barley at the edge. Then the little Ginge brook and its hollow of elms and ash trees interrupted the road. But a few yards beyond it was clear again where the hard road went at right angles away from it to Red Barn. It was now above its green bank, and this was eight or ten feet high with blackthorns on it. It curved slightly round the southern base of Roundabout Hill between the stubble, and being joined by a track from the south it was worn almost grassless. After crossing a track to Ardington, it was slightly raised above the fields on both sides. A hard road joined it, and it was hardened itself and had a line of young beeches and elms on each side. This was to lead up to one of the gates of Lockinge Park, which it entered and disappeared. It must have been bent—probably southward—by the swelling land of the park, but over two centuries of ploughing have left nothing of it visible on the surface.

I turned sharply southward at the edge of this park and presently back to the north-west, past a house of great size with some conservatories, elms, lawns, and water garden—the shadowy and bright grass occupied at that hour by a lap-dog and many swallows. The road, lined on both sides by trees and overhung by valerian and rose-of-Sharon, had an unpleasant sense of privacy meant for others.

The turning eastward out of this road by East Lockinge post office was in line with Ickleton Street, but signs of an exit from the park on the opposite side of the road were obliterated by cottages and gardens. This turning I took, and when it curved decidedly to the right a footpath on the left, between a hedge and some allotment gardens, preserved its original line. This path led westward into a road coming south from Goddard's Barn. On the right-hand side of the entering of the path into this road lay the good house of West Lockinge Farm, its barn and sheds and lodges gathered about it on one side of the road, and its ricks and

Port Way, Wantage.

elm trees opposite. The road was half farm-yard and half road and littered with straw and husks, where the fowls were stalking and pecking with a laziness that seemed perfectly suited to a Sunday early morning following a blazing harvest Saturday.

I hoped to find a cart track going west from the other side of this road. For about a quarter of a mile I thought I found it raised a little in the stubble.

It had been sown and reaped like the rest of the field, but it was a little weedier and grassier. It was making over the swelling arable for Lark Hill and the south edge of Wantage, but I could not find it in the clover nor in the barley beyond that. I therefore turned north into Round Hill, a straight piece of hard road going west into Wantage, with no hedges but grassy borders between it and the arable on either side. This may be the Icknield Way or its successor. It led into the main road at the edge of Wantage, and this I followed into the town. In the first few yards I noticed the sign of the "Lord Nelson" on the left. I recognized it as the work of that venerable artist who designs the faces of guys and turnip-men all over the country. I could tell that the man upon the signboard was Nelson because the uniform corresponded to the name painted below. The face was as much like Nelson as King George III, and it was entirely different from that on the other side of the board. Nevertheless, the effort was to be preferred to a more accurate portrait painted by a builder and decorator's man from a picture in a history book. It was an effort to represent an image of a hero. The builder and decorator's man would have aimed simply at reproducing something which impressed him because it was in a printed book: his horses do not represent what he knows or feels about horses, but what he is able to crib from a photographer in a book advertising somebody's food or embrocation; his "Coach and Horses" is painful to see, because it ought obviously to be in a book.

May it be long before he is allowed to molest the shape of the horse or dragon carved into the turf of White Horse Hill. In its present shape it could not be used to advertise horse food or embrocation: but the horse above Alton Priors could be so used and doubtless one day will be.

As I was leaving Wantage I heard a blackbird singing in a garden beyond the church. This was near the middle of August and a full month since I had last heard one. The heat had dried up the birds' songs all much earlier than usual, and now the rain of the last night seemed to be reviving one. The song was perfect and as strange a thing as last year's snow.

Crossing the Letcombe brook I was out again between hedges and in the company of telegraph posts on the road to Ashbury, Bishopstone, and Swindon, which is called in the inch Ordnance Map "Roman Way." It seemed the only continuation of Ickleton Street, and as there was no other road with anything like the same course in the valley I had little doubt that it was the "Icleton-way" of the early eighteenth century going "all under the hills between them and Childrey, Sparsholt and Uffington, so under White Horse Hill, leaving Woolston and Compton on the right, thence to Ashbury and Bishopston." The foot of the Downs was about a mile on the left, and between them and the road the cornland dipped considerably. Looking over the hedge I saw first a broad land of grass and then a line of telegraph wires making for Letcombe and dividing the grass from a broad band of ripe corn; beyond that was a band of very green roots; then a band of newly ploughed earth; then stubble dappled with dark corn stacks, and above them the hill.

My road was a narrow one, and at first borderless and worn to some depth below the neighbouring fields. At the top of its ascent out of Wantage it had a bank on the right, a fence on the left instead of hedges. After passing Ickleton House at a right-hand turning, I reached two cottages on the right at the crossing of a road from Faringdon to Letcombe. This I entered on the south side to look for a road between mine and the hills. A parish boundary follows this road, and also the lane which I turned into on the right almost at once. The lane was green and ran under some beeches and a natural turf wall south-westward. It was deep worn and rutted as it descended through the corn and barley to a cross-track under another turf wall making from Letcombe Regis Church to Childrey. I went on until my track became a hard road to Lambourn, and as I had seen no sign of an alternative to the "Roman Way," I turned to the right and entered it again at the crossing for Childrey and Letcombe Bassett. Elms clustered at the crossing, and the road was deeply worn between grassy banks. It continued to have hardly any green edge, and as it was usually rising or falling it was sunk more or less below its original level; in one place, for example, the left bank was nearly twenty feet high, and I could see nothing but the clouds all sopped in sunlight. The land was almost entirely arable on either side, with standing corn or stooks or

Under White Horse Hill.

stubble. In one place, past the turning on the right to Westcott, which is between Sparsholt and

Kingston Lisle, the road was on a terrace, having a bank on the left and falling on the right to corn and a thatched farm under trees: there were elms and beeches on either side, but no hedge. The trees of Lisle Park gave lines of handsome beeches to either side of the road, trees of less than a hundred years, all well-shaped and, in fact, almost uniform, and planted at reasonable intervals. The ridge of the Downs was not a mile distant, and from it the grass of a yellowish green colour undulated without a break to the road, sprinkled with beeches and barred with fir plantations. Past the Blowingstone Hill and the turning to Kingston Lisle these undulations are bare and carved by a steep-walled natural cutting. At this point the top of the Downs was only half a mile away, and thenceforward it was never more than a mile until beyond Bishopstone. Actually the nearest point to the ridge was perhaps where the road twisted sharp to the left to the bottom of a coombe and then sharp back again to get out of it. As the floor of the coombe sloped upwards into the hill, these twists gave a road which was bound to cross it at the lowest possible gradient. The coombe had steep, smooth sides of yellowish grass and a winding flat floor, and through the big scattered thorns and elders of it a track went down to Fawler. The road wound again to round a high bank on the left and again to circumvent a thorny hollow on the right, and soon the White Horse was coming into view. There were woods steep above on the left; there had been hedges on both sides since Blowingstone Hill, often bushy and thick and

Dragon Hill.

overscrambled by climbers, as, for example, near Britchcombe Farm. Here the road had a green, sunken course divided from the hard one by a thicket. This farm-house and its thatched, white-stone dependencies, their trees, their elders and nettles, stood close to the road, but a little back from it and a little above it, under the almost precipitous ash wood of the hill ; and away from it on the other side of the road sloped another coombe of thorns, and also of willows and some water.

A little past Britchcombe Farm the Dragon Hill came in sight above a slope of oats and yellowed grass. Then the road twisted again, left and right, to cross another coombe, grown with larch trees on its lower half and having a pool in it near Woolstone Lodge ; but the upper half bending back under the Dragon Hill, with a few thorns on its steep and furrowed walls. Rising up out of the coombe, as usual the road was between steep banks, and on them thorn bushes, scabious, and meadow crane's-bill flowers.

At the crossing to Shrivenham and Lambourn I caught sight of the crest and haggard beech clump of Barbury above the nearer hills. This crossing was within a quarter of a mile of Compton Beauchamp, the last of more than half a dozen villages which the road passed by on its right hand without touching. Ashbury was the first village traversed by the road since Upton. As I approached Ashbury through corn that now ran right to the top of the Downs, I had a bank above me on the left and one below me on the right, and I could see now both Liddington

Green Terrace, near Ashbury

and Barbury clumps, and to the left of Liddington one high, bare breast of turf. A lesser road turned down to Odstone Farm, which I was very glad to see again, not a quarter of a mile on my right—its five plain windows in a row, two in the roof, and those below not to be counted because of the garden shrubs. It was a grey, stone house with a steep, grey roof and a chimney stack at either side; there were elms behind it, and tiled and thatched sheds all on its right hand; and the road going straight down to its left side.

The right-hand hedge gave way to show me the elms and thatched barns and ricks of Ashbury, its church tower among trees rather apart and nearer the Downs. The road descended under a steep left-hand bank, with a green course parallel. It turned right and then left round some elm trees and past a hollow on the right containing a broad millpond enclosed in a parallelogram of elms. At Ashbury the road turned to the right away from the church to the "Rose and Crown," and the two elm trees standing in mid-street, and then back again to the left into its original line. But parallel with the road a footpath ran from the church on a terrace just wide enough for a waggon. It had a green wall above and below, grass on the left, sweet-smelling lucerne on the right. It rose and fell more than the road as it made for Idstone between the barley. The terrace seemed to be continued across the deeply worn road from Swinley Down; but the path turned to the right and into the main road. This terrace road seemed to be a very possible course for an old, though perhaps only an alternative road.

I stopped for a little time at Ashbury, and asking for tea at a cottage and shop combined, I was asked into a silent but formidable Sunday assembly of three incompatible and hostile but respectful generations: a severe but cheerful grandmother in black and spectacles with one finger still marking a place in the Bible; a preoccupied, morose mother, also in black; a depressed but giddy daughter fresh from the counter of a London shop, and already wondering what she was going to do at Ashbury. This girl poured out my tea and told me that there were some very good apples on the tree next door. Neither she nor her relatives, because it was Sunday, could buy these or in any way procure them, so she told me, though she had begun to want them very much after half a day at her native village; if I went—and there seemed no objection to the damnation of a casual wayfarer—I could probably get some. The old lady who lived in the cottage next door said, as if she were stating a well-known fact in the natural history of Ashbury, that she had no apples, that they were very troublesome to knock down, that none had fallen from the trees during the day, and that—she was perfectly certain—there would be none until the morrow. On the morrow I hoped to be many miles from Ashbury, and so I wished her a good afternoon in spite of the rigid sabbatarianism of her trees. I returned to the cottage where I had been drinking tea and told the girl that no apples would fall until Monday morning, and asked her if she knew any other kind of apple trees in Ashbury. Perhaps it was as well that she did not, for I found that Sunday's tea cost twice as much as Saturday's or Monday's—it being apparently the right of the righteous to prey upon the damned, even if in so doing they put themselves into a position apparently as graceless as that of the damned. I thought of asking a clergyman if this was so, and seeing a man whom I took to be a clergyman, because his collar was fastened behind instead of in front, I walked after him. But he suddenly stopped and went into the very cottage of the old lady whose apples would not fall before Monday morning, and this looked so like a conspiracy that I hastened away, glad to have made these discoveries in the natural history of Ashbury.

The deeply worn road from Swinley Down cut across my road, south of the green terrace road, at Idstone, and sent it northwards twenty yards or so, just as Akeman Street cutting across the Upper and Lower Icknield Ways near Tring sent each nearly a mile northwards. After this I could see no trace of the little terrace road, though it was possibly marked by a bank dividing the next fields to the road from those beyond, and then by a mere division between crops to a point above or beyond Bishopstone. Half-way between Idstone and Bishopstone the road entered Wiltshire without ceremony. At the turning just before reaching Bishopstone the road was worn very deep, and above it a steep-walled, bare coombe ran up into the Downs with a track along its edge. More often than not after leaving Wantage the road had been worn thus deep, because it traversed a country of numerous and abrupt undulations; these made fairly steep ascents and descents necessary, and they

Coombe at Bishopstone.

invariably mean the hollowing out of any unmetalled, i.e. of any ancient and not Roman road. The plough could never do any harm to this road. But the "Port Way" between Wantage and Streatley it could hide from most eyes in a few seasons. The

Ickleton Street between Upton and Lockinge Park would almost disappear under a single ploughing, and doubtless often has done so, to reappear in the same or a parallel course when needed.

At Bishopstone the road twisted right and left almost as at Ashbury. This was into a coombe with a little stream in it, and there were some signs that the old way had rather been left and right—that is, sloping down to the ascending bottom of the coombe and up again—as in other coombes. But the coombe and the bare Downs about it were so shaped by nature, by wearing, and apparently by deliberate but inexplicable cutting, that a mere road could not be traced with certainty. The coombe branched as it rose up into the Downs and formed several enormous convexities and concavities of turf. Several of their converging slopes were cut evenly into three or four, or nearly a dozen, green terraces like staircases, all of which, had a company of giants sat there, would have given a view of the spring-head below.

Sheep were strewn over some of these terraces, making arrangements of white dots of a fascinating irregularity. Unless it has become a trick, only a great artist could make similar arrangements of equal beauty. The unknown laws which produce these inevitable accidents are great managers of the beautiful. The succession of bays in an island coast and the general form of the island itself—of course, particularly of islands off our own coast—are beautiful in their way. The shape of England and Wales, the shape of Ireland, of Man, and of the whole flock of the Hebrides please me with their unity, fascinate me with their complexity; a mistaken map of any such known place is as bad æsthetically as geographically. Children are fond of inventing islands with marvellous inlets more romantic than anything on the west coast of Scotland or Scandinavia. But I have never seen one of these invented islands that I could like apart from its creator, or its names, or its sites marked "Buried gold," and so on. They are incredible and raise no wonder. They are not masters' work. I do not know if geologists can support me, but Leonardo's Cave in "The Virgin of the Rocks" always makes me uneasy by what seems to me to be its artificial impossibility. Another great picture which is, I think, faulty in a similar way reminds me of another beauty—the beauty of the scattering and gathering of the stars. I never look at Titian's "Bacchus and Ariadne" without feeling the constellation in that glorious purple is an unhappy invention. It may be my poor astronomy, but I should be inclined to say that stars never could be spread exactly as they are in that picture. It is not merely that there is (I believe) no such constellation, but that the form is one which, for some reason, they would avoid, though by picking a star here and a star there it might be patched up. Birds always fly and fishing-boats always sail in these just patterns. Some are so just that, like that of the sheep above Bishopstone, I should like to have them copied on paper to look at for their mystical arithmetic.

The village, the mill, and the church were lower down to the right below the spring, on the modern road and its northward branches. Only a cottage, with a thatched roof on a level with my feet, lay near the green coombe track above the water. The road went on again between corn and roots, westwards now, and gradually farther from the Downs, until a cross-road from Bourton cut across it and sent it southwards a quarter-mile by a willowy spring before it turned west again.

This road southward into the Marlborough and Hungerford road may yet be shown to be part of the Icknield Way. For at Totterdown, a mile and a half beyond, it curves round and makes a line with the road to Chisledon under Liddington Hill—the road much resembling the Icknield Way which is called "Ridgeway" on the maps. It rose now, a hedged and elmy road, to five hundred feet, and had a deep, grassy hollow and elm trees below, between it and the cornland of the Downs. It dipped to a spring and a post office at Hinton Parva; it dipped again and rose to a view over the northern vale to the dim, watery wall of the Cotswolds. At this height it crossed Ermine Street just after passing a "Black Horse." All four ways at the crossing were deeply worn and made a pit with bushy banks and tiny green triangles of waste in the midst.

In a quarter-mile past the crossing of Ermine Street I was at Wanborough. There the road forked at the "Calley Arms." There is not a scrap of real or pretended documentary evidence for either road, at least until the place-names mentioned in the Saxon charter relating to Wanborough have been identified. The left-hand road had the advantage of keeping near the hills, instead of going clean away west like the right-hand one. This right-hand road may at last be connected with one of those rumoured roads going westwards, under the secondary line of chalk hills, past Holy Cross at Swindon, past Elcombe and Studley to St. Anne's-in-the-Wood at Brislington, in Somerset, or to Devonshire; and this continuation may at last be shown to be entitled to the name of Icknield Way. I followed the left-hand road because it seemed possible to connect it with one, very much like the Icknield Way and in a similar relation to the Downs, going south-westward through Wroughton and Broad Hinton, and from there either to Avebury or to Yatesbury, and so by Juggler's Lane to Cherhill on its way to Bath.

Liddington clump, the straight ridge and the "castle" rampart upon it, were clear ahead as I took this turning. Wanborough's towered and spired church stood at the top of a slope of grass on my right. It was a crooked, hedged road, with a grassy edge and a path on the grass; and the telegraph posts followed it. It passed out of Wanborough parish at a tiny stream that crossed the road in a deep, narrow cleft with willows and willow herbs below on the right, and in the widening cleft a derelict mill, a steep garden plot, and a row of beehives. It rose up narrow, deep, and steep to the "Bell" at Liddington. There I turned to the left into the Swindon road, and almost at once to the left again, leaving the church on my left. This took me past two or three houses of Medbourne, and sharp to the left and right through the hamlet of Badbury, where a great elm stands at the first turning above a deep hollow and a road going northward down it to the right. Then crossing the Roman road from Mildenhall to Wanborough Nythe, I was at Chisledon and another cleft in the land. This cleft is often precipitous, and so narrow that you could almost play cards across it. A streamlet and a single line of railway wind along the bottom. The church stands at the edge where it is gentler, and the village is scattered over the slopes and edges.

I was hungry when I knocked at the door of the first inn at half-past five. On the opposite side of the road a small, quiet crowd of drinkers in black coats and hats waited to be let in at six. No one answered my knock. I knocked louder, and still louder, on the woodwork of the door. Then I rapped the glass, and rapped louder and many times. But no one came, and as I was too hungry to want justice I went to the next inn. Here the door was instantly opened by a little red-faced landlady with fuzzy hair and a gnomish face. She was swift and clean, and so light and quick was her step that every time I heard her approaching I expected a child. She was sorry to say that she had no bed to spare, but told me of someone that might. I tried in vain, then called opposite where "refreshments" were advertised. An enormous woman stood wedged in the doorway ; she was black-haired, sullen, and faintly moustached, and she had her hands hanging down because there was no room on either side of her to clasp them, and no room in the doorway for her to rest them upon the fat superincumbent upon her hips. I said good evening, and she remained silent. I asked her if she had a bed to spare. She looked me up and down with a movement of head and eyes, and asked me gradually where I came from. I was so taken aback that I told her like a child, " From East Hendred "—which was absurd. She retreated to ask her husband. He appeared alone, and hanging down his head, shook it, and said that he did not think he could spare me a bed. Having no gift of speech, I turned very rapidly away from him and back to the inn. The landlady thought of someone else, made inquiries, and assured me that the bed would be ready when Mrs. Somebody got back from church. So I went out and looked at Burderop, Ladder Hill, and the turning " To the Downs and Rockley." The woman was back from church and opened the door to me. She had a background of women taking off Sunday hats and putting away veils and prayer-books, and said she was sorry, but a niece had come, and there was no room for me. In the darkening street I saw an old man at a gate with a genial face and the mouth of one accustomed to horses. I asked him if he knew of a bed to spare. " No—oh–oh–oh—no," he chuckled, with increased geniality. " You've come to the wrong place. . . . Oh–ho–ho–ho–ho no," he continued. " I can't tell you why; but if you want a bed you have to go to a town." He was only a visitor to Chisledon, and I wished him better treatment than I had got. I set out for Swindon. In about a mile I came to another inn, where I had always enjoyed the bread and cheese and ale, and I unwillingly silenced a black-coated company of grave drinkers standing at the bar. They suspended their glasses while the landlord said that it was absolutely impossible to get a bed that side of Swindon. I tried at Coate. The barmaid appealed to Mr. MacFaggart, who was standing by—"Perhaps Mrs. MacFaggart can spare a bed?" "No." This series of refusals was, I am convinced, pure ill-luck. But the stout woman refused me, almost beyond doubt, because I was a stranger whom she could not immediately classify. I could not be classed as a "gentleman," as a young "gent" or "swell," or as a plain "young fellow." She decided not to risk it. Perhaps she had savings about the house. Or did she think that underneath less than two days' beard, that oldish and not very clean Burberry waterproof, those good but very baggy trousers, murder was lurking? No, probably she felt not the very slightest inclination to please me, and as it only meant half a crown, her one difficulty in refusing was her natural sullenness increased by the presence of the nondescript and unsympathetic casual stranger on a Sunday. Country people know a country gentleman, a sporting financier, a tradesman, a young townsman (clerk or artisan), a working man, and a real tramp or roadster. Some of them know the artist or distinguished foreigner, with a foot of hair, broad-brimmed hat, and corduroy or soft tweeds, a cloak and an ostentatious pipe, tasselled, or of enormous bulk, or elaborate form or unusual substance. Some know the hairy and hygienic man in sandals. To be elbowed out at nightfall after a day's walking by an unconscious conspiracy of a whole village was enough to produce either a hate of Chisledon or a belief that the devil or a distinguished relative was organizing the opposition. But during those four unexpected miles to Swindon in the volcanic heat of evening, which produced several pains and a constant struggle between impatient mind and dull, tired body, I felt chiefly: I suffer ; I do not want to suffer ; and only now and then the face of Mrs. Stout, or of Mrs. Smallbeer, or of the genial old man with the horsy mouth, came into my head, and turned my depression to fury.

Possibly they were afraid of German spies at Chisledon. Not far from Maidstone in the summer of 1910 some poor cottage children were telling me how a German spy wanted to rob them of the lunch they were taking to school. He was a dark stranger with a beard, and he was waiting about at a crossing partly overhung by trees ; and they were convinced that he wished to steal their food, and that his reason for doing so was his position as German spy.

At Swindon I felt what a man feels in a place where he knows one man instead of knowing scores of children and feeling that every passing stranger was of the same family, ready at a touch to be changed to a friend. But I had no difficulty in finding a bed surrounded by the following decorations: pictures of ships in quiet and in roaring seas; of roses twining about the words, "The Lord shall be thy everlasting light"; of a cart-horse going through a ford with three children on his back; of an Italian boatman and three buxom girls, one clinking glasses with him; advertisements of an aperient and of cheap cigarettes. The advertisement of cigarettes dwarfed all the rest. For not only was the lettering large, but there was also a coloured picture of a swarthy and hearty woman practically naked to the waist. She was smiling with her dark eyes, and her lips were parted. I could not imagine what she had to do with cigarettes of any kind. Was there a kind of suggestion that these bold, bad, under-dressed foreign beauties—undoubtedly beauties—were capable of smoking the cigarettes? Or was the picture meant to be a stimulus to some, a satisfaction to others, of those who sat at their ease drinking and smoking and thinking of women? In the tap-room of the most rustic public houses two or three of these women sometimes adorn the walls, along with a picture of a diseased cow and of its mouth, stomach, and udder. Some are dark, some are fair, and, I think, certainly meant to be English; but all are incompletely draped and unashamed. The dark ones are vaunting heathen beauties, the fair tend to be insipid, with expressions borrowed from the pious virgins of religious pictures. Sometimes the Bacchante and the pious virgin are to be seen side by side, the sacred one being supplied by the village grocer at Christmas. They are equally beautiful, i.e. have regular features, perfect complexions, and expressionless mouths, and are doing nothing in particular except posing so that the artist shall observe their bosoms, or, in the case of sacred pictures, their throats and the whites of their eyes. I do not think it could be shown that these pictures spoil the chances of girls with unclassical features and cross-eyes in the villages. In these matters the moth that desires the star is likely to end in a candle flame, whether or not he mistook it for a star. In these new towns I see women looking as if they were made in the chemists' shops, which are so numerous and conspicuous in the streets—thin, pallid, dyspeptic, vampirine beauties, having nothing but sex in common with the bold, swarthy alien on the cigarette advertisement. . . .

At Swindon the explorer of the Icknield Way has all the world before him. He may go through Marlborough into the Pewsey Valley, and either along under the hills through Lavington to Westbury, or, turning out of the Pewsey Valley, to Old Sarum, and beyond Westbury or Sarum into the extreme west; and he will be on a road of the same type as the Icknield Way for the greater part of the distance. Or he may content himself with reaching Avebury. Or he may miss Avebury and aim at Bath. At present documents and traditions keep a perfect silence west of Wanborough, and among mere possibilities the choice is endless. The easiest, the pleasantest, and the wrongest thing to do is to take to the Ridgeway at Wanborough and follow it along the supposed south-westerly course under Liddington Hill, under Barbury Castle, and then up on to the ridge to Avebury. But though it is possible that in the Middle Ages this was done, there is little doubt that the green way going high up on the ridge past Glory Ann Barn is not coeval with, is not the same road as, the hill-foot road that has crept persistently but humbly under the Chilterns and Berkshire Downs. Such a road ran more risks than the Ridgeway from the plough. Its preservation between Upton and Lockinge Park is miraculous. It might easily have disappeared in the ploughland about Chisledon or the rich pastures of Coate. Let the conjecturer thus skip a few miles in his westerly or south-westerly course, and he can go rapidly ahead, following under the main ridge to Avebury, or under the secondary ridge, three or four miles north of it, towards Calne and Bath. It is a game of skill which deserves a select reputation—to find an ancient road of the same character as the Oxfordshire and Berkshire Icknield Way, going west or south-west beyond Wanborough. The utmost reward of this conjecturing traveller would be to find himself on the banks of the Towy or beside the tomb of Giraldus at St. David's itself.

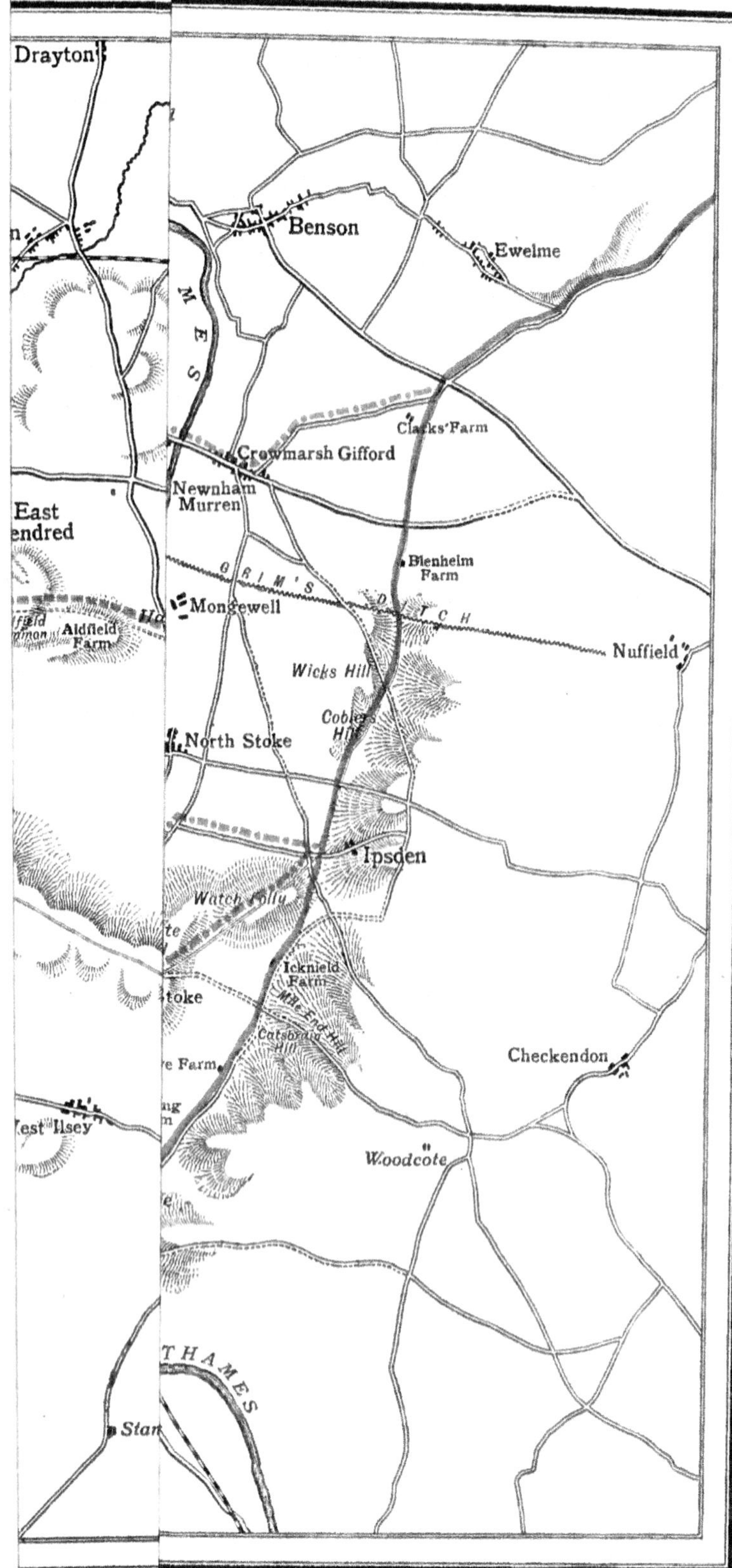

Drayton
Benson
Ewelme
Crowmarsh Gifford
Clacks' Farm
Newnham
Murren
East
endred
Blenheim
Farm
G R I M ' S D I T C H
Mongewell
Aldfield
Farm
Nuffield
Wicks Hill
North Stoke
Ipsden
Watch Folly
Icknield
Farm
Mile End Hill
Catsbrain
Hill
toke
Checkendon
Woodcote
West Ilsey
THAMES

INDEX

WILLIAM BRENDON AND SON, LTD. PRINTERS, PLYMOUTH

Lightning Source UK Ltd.
Milton Keynes UK
UKOW05f1918171016

285508UK00017B/442/P